American History Stories...
...you never read in school
...but should have.

Volume II: We the People

REPRINTED FROM THE ORIGINAL
SCHOOL TEXTBOOK OF 1890

By Mara L. Pratt, M.D.
with an Introduction by
Reed R. Simonsen

FIRST PRINTING

On the Cover: "Divide and Conquer."
   Copyright 1997 Tom W. Freeman, courtesy of SM&S
Naval Prints, Inc. All rights reserved. Those wishing to
acquire a print may write: SM&S Naval Prints, Inc.
P.O. Box 41, Forest Hill, MD 21050-0041 or call
1-888-215-9403.

I.S.B.N. 0-9640546-1-2

Never have such simple words captured the heart and soul of a nation. Where, in all of history, have there been a people so in touch with humanity as to have understood that men are, and by divine right have always been, free and equal under heaven. As our founders declared their liberty in the Declaration of Independence, they wrote down a morality that would shake the world.

We hold these Truths to be self-evident, that all Men are created equal, that they are endowed by their Creator with certain unalienable Rights, that among these are Life, Liberty and the Pursuit of Happiness -- That to secure these Rights, Governments are instituted among Men, deriving their just Powers from the Consent of the Governed...

Human history is full of tyrants, social architects and petty scientists who have insisted that man exists to serve the state. They have long declared that freedom comes from collective law and that rights are granted by governments. They were wrong then, and they are wrong now. Human rights come from the Creator and governments exist solely to secure these rights.

It is true that as a nation we have struggled. Occasionally, we have forgotten our ideals. At times, the majority has stepped upon the necks of the minority. At other times, a single individual has tramped the rights of millions. Once or twice we have compromised the people's sovereignty through dangerous and sticky treaties or foreign relations. But America, despite her learning curve, eventually finds her way back. We are the grand experiment in freedom. We have no guide book but our history and our common faith in our national motto. "In God we trust." These will see us through.

Freedom is a balancing act. It is checked by laws, balanced by morality and protected by gridlock. As a people we have not done everything right, but we have done more right than wrong. We the People have been great when we have been true to our founding principles. We have only faltered when we have betrayed ourselves.

We owe it to our ancestors to preserve these memories and awaken them anew in the heart and soul of each emerging generation. Let us teach them truth, right and honor, and thereby save ourselves and all the world from slavery. May we stand united. May we yet remain, We the People.

Reed R. Simonsen

ABOUT THE ARTIST

A native of Pontiac, Michigan, Tom W. Freeman developed his skill early. He achieved national recognition for his work in an exhibition held for the International Red Cross when still in his teens. A self-taught artist, Tom has worked as an illustrator for the Marines and Army. His art has been featured in numerous books and magazines, fine-art prints and posters, porcelain plaques and plates. His paintings can be seen in galleries internationally, in the Presidential West Wing of the White House and on permanent exhibit at the Arizona Memorial in Honolulu, Hawaii.

CONTENTS.

	PAGE.
The Nation,	5
The First President,	7
The Installation of Washington (*Illustration*),	9
Washington's Administration,	13
Washington's Thought for Others,	16
Washington's Grave, Mount Vernon (*Illustration*),	17
The Whiskey Insurrection,	18
Washington as a Fighter,	20
John Adams' Administration,	23
Administration of Thomas Jefferson,	27
Duel Between Hamilton and Burr (*Illustration*),	30
Jefferson and Randolph,	34
Jefferson's Fiddle, .	36
The Administration of James Madison,	38
Dolly Madison,	41
The War of 1812,	43
Impressment of American Sailors (*Illustration*),	45
Hull's Surrender of Detroit,	48
The American Army of Two,	50
The Constitution and the Guerriere	54
Old Ironsides (*Poetry*), .	57
The Wasp and the Frolic	58
The Lost War Sloop (*Poetry*),	60
"Don't Give Up the Ship" .	62
Fight Between the "Chesapeake" and "Shannon," (*Illustration*), .	64
"Remember the River Raisin"	70
Our Capital Taken by the English	74

CONTENTS.

The End of the War	78
The Attack on New Orleans	79
The Era of Good Feeling	80
President Monroe (*Illustration*),	81
J. Q. Adams (*Illustration*),	84
Evils of Early Rising	86
President Jackson (*Illustration*),	87
Andrew Jackson	88
Henry Clay (*Illustration*),	90
Andrew Jackson's Nick-name	92
Jackson's Obstinacy,	93
General Jackson's Portrait,	94
Calhoun at Home,	96
Daniel Webster (*Illustration*),	98
The Home of Webster,	99
Daniel Webster's Fishing,	101
Van Buren,	103
"Tippecanoe & Tyier too,"	104
President Tyler (*Illustration*),	106
A Small-Tail Movement,	107
James K. Polk,	109
Captain Fremont (*Illustration*),	114
General Winfield Scott (*Illustration*),	116
The Angels of Buena Vista (*Poetry*),	117
The Martyr of Monterey (*Poetry*),	119
Zachary Taylor,	121
Zachary Taylor (*Illustration*),	123
James Buchanan, Millard Fillmore (*Illustrations*),	124
The Abolitionists,	125
John G. Whittier (*Illustration*),	128
The Fugitive Slave Law,	129
John Brown,	131
John Brown (*Illustration*),	132
Harper's Ferry,	134
Brown of Ossawatomie (*Poetry*),	137
Presidents of the United States (*Poetry*),	139

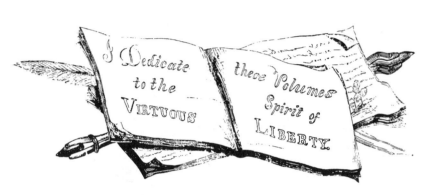

THE CAPITOL, WASHINGTON.

AMERICAN HISTORY STORIES.

II.

THE NATION.

In all the history of our people up to
this time, you have heard always
the terms *colonies* and *colonists;*
but now, after the Revolution,
these colonists re-organized themselves
under a new government, with a
President at the head. They now called the different
colonies *States*, and spoke of themselves henceforth as the
American Nation.

For a long time after the Revolution, the kind of government they should have was a question of great dispute.
Some would have liked a government similar to that of
England, with a king at the head; others declared they
would have nothing like the English government, and were
especially determined never again to be ruled by a king —
not even a king of their own choosing.

Finally, in 1787, a convention of fifty of the leading men of the country met at Philadelphia to decide upon some form of government which should, as nearly as possible, suit all the colonies.

For four whole months they worked together, and at last presented to the people the "Constitution," as it was called, which to this day forms the basis of our government.

Of course, this constitution, wise as it was, could not suit everybody. Franklin himself, who was one of the fifty who wrote it, was not entirely satisfied with it; but, with each of the thirteen colonies wanting something different from every other, it was the best that they could do. On the whole, it gave very good satisfaction; ten of the colonies — States, I should say now — accepted it at once. Three States, however, held out against it for some time. But two of them gave way without much trouble. Rhode Island, the smallest State of all — so small that it is called Little Rhody — then stood alone, stoutly refusing for a year or more to come into the ranks. This shows, I suppose, that even the little Rhodys and little Johnnies may be as plucky as the larger ones, if only they believe they are in the right. Little Rhody, however, finally gave way, and entered the Union with the same good will to all, no doubt, that had been shown by the other States.

Now a flag — the United States Flag — with its thirteen stars and thirteen stripes — was unfurled to the breezes; and the colonies were indeed the "United States of America."

THE FIRST PRESIDENT.

When, at last, the States had all agreed to accept the Constitution as the basis of government, the next thing to do was to elect a President, and so establish themselves as the American Nation at once.

As might be expected, Washington was the man chosen for this important office ; and when we recall how generous, how brave, and how wise he had been during the Revolution, we cannot doubt for a moment that he was the very best choice for this new position.

It was decided to make New York City the capital of the United States ; and thither Washington in his coach-and-four set forth from his beautiful home in Virginia to take his place as first President of the United States of America. It is said that his journey was one ovation from the time he left Mt. Vernon (his home) until he reached New York City. Crowds of gaily-dressed people, bearing baskets and wreaths of flowers, hailed his appearance at every village, with shouts and songs of joy.

When he reached Trenton — the very place where, a few years before, so heartsick and discouraged he had crossed the Delaware on that wintry Christmas night to attack the drunken Hessians,— at this very place the road was strewn with roses, the young maidens held arches of flowers over him, and the air rang with songs of gratitude and welcome.

In New York City a grand ball was given. Never before had this little community seen so much elegance. Washington had left off his blue "soldier coat," and was now dressed in a handsome suit of black velvet, with white silk stockings, beautiful silver buckles, and satin waistcoat. He was very tall, and straight, and manly looking; and with his elegant dress, and his powdered hair, he must indeed have made a very distinguished appearance.

John Adams, the Vice-president, was there, and so was Hamilton, the Secretary of the Treasury. General Knox, too, with his beautiful wife — the most beautiful woman of her time, so it is said, was there. Jefferson, who had been in France some time, now came back to America to be present at this "Inauguration Ball." He took everybody by surprise by appearing dressed as were the French people at that time — in white broadcloth coat, scarlet waistcoat and breeches, cocked hat, and white stockings. It was indeed a wonderful ball, and I am sure there were beauty, and elegance, and grace, such as any court in Europe might well have been proud of.

In all the large towns celebrations of all sorts were held. In the city of New York there was a grand procession, such as never before had been seen in America. This procession was headed by a man dressed to look like Columbus, the discoverer of the country. Behind him were long lines of men with axes, who represented the pioneers — that is,

THE INSTALLATION OF WASHINGTON.

the men who first came here from Europe, and felled the trees and cleared the places for roads and cities ; then came lines of men dressed to represent the farmers, with plows, and scythes, and reapers ; then came carts, fitted up like work-shops to represent the different trades. One cart, which represented a bake-shop, had upon it a huge loaf of bread, ten feet high, on which were printed the names of all the states ; the coopers were putting together a barrel with thirteen staves, and binding it with a strong iron band, which they called "The New Constitution ; " the butchers were roasting a whole ox, which, when the celebration was over, was to be eaten by the people in the procession.

In the procession there were thirteen boys, each thirteen years old, dressed in white, with ribbons and garlands of green.

On another cart was a printing press ; and, as it passed along, the printers printed copies of patriotic verses, and flung them right and left to the people.

Greatest of all, was a big ship — the "Ship of State " — drawn by ten large milk-white horses. O, it was a grand day for New York ! The people shouted and hurrahed till they were hoarse ; and, at last, when the procession had been everywhere and had been seen by everybody, all went into a great tent, decorated with flags and banners, where the women of the city had prepared a feast for them ; then they shouted and hurrahed more, listened to speeches, drank toasts to the "new Government" and to the "new President," and finally went to their different homes, prouder than ever, I've no doubt, of the new "American Nation."

We hear in these days a great deal of fault found over the manner in which our Presidents from time to time choose their aids. It is often said, perhaps unjustly, that they are chosen with very little regard to their fitness for the offices which they are to fill, but rather because they chance to be friends or relations, or to have some other claim upon the president.

Whether this is so or not, Washington certainly set for all his successors a glorious example in this one line.

During his administration as President of the United States, a gentleman, a friend of the President throughout the whole course of the Revolutionary war, applied for a certain office. The gentleman was at all times welcome to Washington's table. He had been, to a certain degree, necessary to the man who had for seven years fought the battles of his country. At all times and in all places Washington regarded his Revolutionary associate with an eye of partiality and confidence.

He was a jovial, pleasant, companion; and in applying for the office, his friends already cheered him in his prospect of success.

The opponent of this gentleman was known to be an enemy of Washington. He dared, however, to stand as a candidate for the office to which the friend and favorite of Washington aspired.

Every one considered the appointment of this man hopeless. No flattering testimonial of merit had he to present to the eye of Washington. He was known to be his political enemy. He was opposed by a favorite of the General; and yet with such fearful odds he dared to stand as a candidate. What was the result? The enemy of Washington was appointed to the office, and his table companion left destitute and rejected.

A mutual friend, who interested himself in the affair, ventured to remonstrate with the President for the injustice of his appointment. "My friend," said he, "I receive with a cordial welcome. He is welcome to my house and welcome to my heart. But, with all his good qualities, he is not a man of business. His opponent is, with all his political hostility to me, a man of business. My private feelings have nothing to do in this case. I am not George Washington, but President of the United States. As George Washington, I would do this man any kindness in my power; but as the President of the United States I can do nothing."

WASHINGTON'S ADMINISTRATION.

Ad-min-is-trá-tion is a large word, perhaps you think. But, after all, it isn't very much larger than Revolution, or Constitution; and when you come to know what it means, and why we have to use it, you will find it just as easy as many words which are perhaps not quite so long.

While a President holds his office we speak of it as his administration; and those events which occur while a certain person is President, are always spoken of as the events of that President's administration.

Although it was no doubt a great honor to have been chosen first President of the United States, and although it must have been very pleasant to Washington to know that his people so loved and trusted him, still he knew there was hard, hard work ahead, and no little worriment; for, although the States had accepted the Constitution, still there were persons here and there who still clung to the idea of having each State rule itself without any President at all or any Congress; others there were, who had wanted a king and who would have much preferred to keep the government out of the hands of the common people. All these critics were of course watching every movement of the new President, ready to find fault, and say, "Just what we expected," if the least thing went wrongly. Then, too, there were other difficulties. The treasury was nearly empty, and no other nation was willing to lend money to this new government; the Indians were rioting, burning and plundering on the frontiers; pirates from the Barbary States were attacking American ships and putting American seamen into prison; Spain had refused to allow the Americans the use of the Mississippi River for their trade; England, too, would not make any treaty of commerce with the new country — and, worst of all, there was the empty treasury — no money with which to raise armies to fight the Indians; no money with which to send ships to attack the Barbary States; no money to offer Spain; no money even with which to pay the old debts of the Revolution. A perplexing place it was, indeed, for Washington and his cabinet. But they were equal to the occasion. Hamilton, the Secretary of the Treasury, managed the money affairs so successfully that he has ever since been held up as an example of wisdom to all succeeding Treasurers. He established a National Bank, and levied taxes in order to raise the money which the government so much needed.

I shall not attempt to tell you how all these things were brought about, for you could not understand it, and it would not be very interesting to you even if you could.

All I want you to remember just now is, that Washington and his Cabinet were very wise in their dealings with all these troubles — so wise that, when, eight years later, Washington retired from public life, the money troubles were greatly improved, the Indians had been held back Spain had been made to allow the Americans the use of the Mississippi, and the Barbary States had given up the prisoners, and had promised not to interfere further with American vessels.

The country, you see, was in a far better condition than it had been when, eight years before, Washington was made President.

As the President's term is four years, Washington had, you will understand, served two terms. As the time for a third election drew near, Washington resigned his office, saying that he had tried to serve his country faithfully through its darkest hours, and that now, being sixty-five years old, he wished to retire to his home at Mt. Vernon and spend the rest of his life in rest and quiet.

There had been on all sides men who said, during Washington's administration, "Washington will be King yet. He means to be King. He will hold his office until he *is* King." But I wonder what these men said when, at the end of the second term, Washington so quietly and modestly retired to his own home, thus proving how little he cared for public life except when his country needed him.

Washington did not live very long after his return to his home. Not many months had passed when there came news of his sudden death.

Every possible honor was paid this brave, good man, the

Father of his Country, as he was called.   In England and France even, the highest honors were paid him.   The English ships were ordered to wear their flags at half mast, and the French ruler ordered that the banners be draped with crape.

Wherever Washington's name was mentioned, it was always with tender reverence and love.

WASHINGTON'S THOUGHT FOR OTHERS.

In no way, perhaps, do we show ourselves to be gentle-bred, more than in our consideration for others.

After Cornwallis had surrendered at Yorktown, he dined one day with Washington.   Rochambeau, the French commander, was also present, and according to the custom, being asked for a toast, he said, "The United States."

Washington, in turn, gave "The King of France."

When Cornwallis's turn came he said, simply, "The King."

— "Of England," added Washington with a smile.   Keep him there, and I'll drink him a full bumper!" — and so saying he filled his glass to overflowing.

WASHINGTON'S GRAVE, MOUNT VERNON.

GEORGE WASHINGTON,
1789–1797.

National Bank.
Terms made with Spain,
Algiers and England.

THE WHISKEY INSURRECTION.

In order to raise money during this trying time in the nation's history, a tax was put upon whiskey and other alcoholic liquors.

This movement met with much rebellion among the people ; and in Pennsylvania there was an open outbreak known as "The Whiskey Insurrection."

During this outbreak, the leader, Bradford, gained great power over a certain wealthy farmer named John Mitchel, and in some underhand manner, drew him into the conspiracy. Mitchel was young and full of vigor, and believed he was doing right.

One night Bradford came to Mitchel and said, "I believe letters have been written, and are now on the way to the President, telling of our plans for insurrection here. Now, those letters someway must be seized. You are the man to do it. As the mail-wagon passes along this road, you are to stop it, get that mail-bag and destroy those letters."

Robbery of the mails was then an offence punishable by death ; but Mitchel, convinced that he was risking his life to serve his country, joined by two other men, stopped the wagon on a lonely road, between Washington and Pittsburgh, and carried the mail-bag to Bradford's house. It was opened, the damaging letters taken out, and the rest returned to the post-office at Pittsburgh.

When the insurrection was over, all the leaders escaped excepting John Mitchel. He rode into camp, and, finding General Morgan, gave himself up.

"I have been a fool," he said. "I see that plainly. I am ready to bear the punishment of my folly."

General Morgan, who knew that he had been deceived by Bradford, was sorry that he had not made his escape with him. He believed Mitchel to be at heart an honest man; and, knowing that if he were brought to trial the punishment would be death, he determined to give him a chance to escape.

"You cannot be tried here," he said. "I will give you a pass to Philadelphia. Report yourself there."

"I am to have a guard?"

"No, none."

The General turned on his heel and walked away. He intended and expected Mitchel to fly as soon as he had reached the wilderness; but the young farmer's honor was a stricter guard than soldiers would have been, and it drove him without flinching to his death.

He bade farewell to his wife and child, and started alone on horseback to Philadelphia. It was a three weeks' journey, at any hour of which he could have escaped. He reported himself as a prisoner, was tried, convicted, and sentenced to be hanged.

When the news reached General Morgan, he sent a

special messenger to the President, with an account of the facts in the case. Washington, it is said, was deeply touched, and at once sent a full pardon to Mitchel, giving him at the same time this fatherly advice : " Go home to your wife and child ; and forevermore keep clear of conspirators. You could hardly expect to escape again, for we are very apt to be judged by the company we keep."

WASHINGTON AS A FIGHTER.

When it was necessary, peace-loving as he was, Washington could fight. His clear sense of the thing that must not be done as well as the thing that must be done, was what made him of such value both as General and as President.

This incident shows his strength, his firmness, and his quickness to act. At one time, Colonel Glover's Marblehead soldiers and Morgan's Virginia riflemen had fallen into a disgraceful quarrel. The Virginians had laughed at the somewhat peculiar dialect and the short round jackets of the fishermen soldiers ; the Marbleheaders, on the other hand, had made fun of the hunting-shirts and leggins of the riflemen.

The two regiments had gone on from words to blows, until at last, as Washington rode up, they were in full riot.

In an instant Washington's practised eye took in the situation. Leaping from his horse, and throwing the bridle to his servant Pompey, who stood near, he dashed into the midst of the fight, seized two of the biggest, brawniest of the riflemen by their throats, and holding them at arm's length, shook them, until with surprise and breathlessness they were glad to cry for quarter.

Then, quietly giving orders that the two men be taken to their camps, and that there should be no more quarreling between the two regiments, he rode away, leaving all — officers and soldiers — blank with amazement at this sudden outburst from their commander-in-chief.

WASHINGTON'S AIDS.

Washington was wise in his choice of men to help him carry on his work as President. He was as wise in his judgment of men, a friend once said of him, as he was in his judgment of horses. As he never trained for the saddle a colt that was fitted to the plow, so he never chose as an aid in government a man who was better fitted for other lines of work.

" In choosing Alexander Hamilton and Col. Meade for his aids," said Col. Meade himself, " Washington displayed his usual good judgment. For Hamilton was a vigorous

writer and a strong thinker. I was only a fearless horse-
man. So you see Hamilton did the headwork and I did
the riding."

At the close of the war, when Washington was taking
leave of his aids, he said : —

"Hamilton, you ought to go to the bar. You might
easily become a leading lawyer. And you, friend Dick,
should go to your plantation. You have it in you to make
a noble, honest farmer — just such a one as our country
needs. It is indeed such men as you that make a country."

Hamilton did become a leader of the New York
Bar, and Meade became the famous plantation holder that
Washington had hoped he might become.

Several years after this, Meade visited Washington at
his home. Washington, gallant host that he was, rode out
to meet him. They met at a pair of draw-bars — one on
either side.

"Allow me to let down the bars," said Meade, "for my
worthy General."

"Friend Dick," said Washington, "here, as your host, it
is *my* privilege to take down the bars."

For an instant both stood, hats in hand, each courte-
ously waiting to serve the other.

Then with the ready wit and hearty manner which
belonged always to Meade, he said, "Very well, General,
then allow me to be your *aid* still."

JOHN ADAMS' ADMINISTRATION.

During the eight years of Washington's administration, so many important matters had come up that the people, by taking sides in the different discussions, had come to form two political parties. They called themselves Federalists and Republicans just as the political parties to-day call themselves Democrats and Republicans. The Federalists were those who believed in having a

JOHN ADAMS.

Congress, and a President who should stand at the head of the government. The Republicans said that was too much like having a king, and they believed that some time the President would become the king. They wanted each State to govern itself separately, have its own officers, and make its own laws. It would be time enough for the States to unite under one leader, so the Republicans said, when there was war, or when some other such matter of general interest came up.

And so it came about that at the end of Washington's administration, when it became necessary to elect a new president, each party had a candidate of its own. It was agreed that the candidate receiving the largest number of votes should be President, and the other one should be Vice-president.

John Adams was selected as candidate by the Federalists, and Thomas Jefferson by the Republicans.

I hardly think it will pay in a little history like this to go into the particulars of the contest. All we need to know now is, that Adams became the next President, and Jefferson the Vice-president. These two men, although bitterly opposed to each other in their political ideas, were nevertheless strong personal friends. During the Revolution they had stood bravely side by side, and after their terms of office had ended, they again became firm friends. It seems quite remarkable that on the 4th of July, 1826, the day when the "Declaration of Independence" was just fifty years old, both these men died.

The last words of John Adams were, "My friend, Thomas Jefferson, still lives." He did not know that Jefferson had died only a few hours before in his Virginia home.

The one thing that marks the administration of John Adams, was the passing of the "Alien and Sedition Laws," as they were called. By these laws, the President had a right to expel from the country any foreigner who seemed dangerous to the country, and to fine or imprison any American who *libelled* the Congress, the President, or the Government.

These laws excited much bitter feeling; for the Republicans at once declared that it was intended to take away their freedom of speech, and that it was but one step towards bringing them all upon their knees before a king. The Federalists, many of them, thought this new law rather too strong, and began to take sides with the Republicans. And so it came about that when Adams's term was out, the Republican party had become so strong that Jefferson was elected the next President.

During the administration of Adams, the country came very near having war with France. Charles Pinckney was sent to France to see what could be done. The French government hinted to Pinckney that if the United States would pay to France a certain amount of money they, the French, would agree to make no trouble for them.

One would suppose the French government would have known better than to make such an offer to a country that had just fought so bravely for her liberty, and had since struggled so hard to meet its honest debts, and make for itself a place among the nations of the world.

Pinckney was very indignant. "No," said he," millions for defence, but not one cent for tribute," was his bold, manly reply.

What the result might have been we cannot tell, had the threatened war burst upon us ; but it happened that matters in Europe took such a turn that France did not carry out its threat against us.

It was during Adams' administration that the capitol was changed from New York to a new city, just laid out on the banks of the Potomac, which had been named Washington.

Here the building for the future presidents of the United States was erected; and President Adams and his good wife went there to begin housekeeping.

Poor Mrs. President had rather a trying time of it. Rough indeed was this new capitol. Except a few public buildings, there was hardly a house in sight. Although wood was plenty, they could hardly find laborers to cut it, and, as Mrs. Adams once wrote to a friend, they were really afraid they could not keep warm enough to drive away the shivers. Such was the Capitol of our country at the beginning of this century.

JOHN ADAMS.
1797–1801.

Alien and Sedition Laws.
War with France threatened.
The New Capitol.

ADMINISTRATION OF THOMAS JEFFERSON.

THOMAS JEFFERSON.

The country had all this time been growing richer and richer. The people were spreading out over the western country, towns were being built, and great tracts of land were being made into thrifty farms. Several new States had already been added to the Union — Vermont, Kentucky, and Tennessee — and now Ohio even, which so short a time before had been but an Indian hunting ground, was added, a new star, to those already upon the Flag.

You remember that Spain had at one time refused the Americans the use of the Mississippi river. They owned the land from the mouth of the river up to the Falls of St. Anthony; and, although agreements had been made with Spain regarding the use of the river, still the United States much preferred to own the land bordering upon it, and so be sure of their control of its navigation.

Spain had, recently ceded all this country, then called
Louisiana, to the French. Jefferson now offered $15,000,-
000 to France for this country, and, as France was greatly
in need of money, the offer was accepted at once. When
asked why he did it, Jefferson said, " There is no trouble
threatened at present, I know ; but I believe in having a
good big country, with no troublesome neighbors at the
back door, as there might have been had the Spaniards or
the French held that country."

Meantime the pirates of the Barbary States were alive
again. They began capturing our vessels, taking our men
prisoners, and selling them as slaves.

It is wonderful how these pirates had frightened the
European nations even, and had kept them in terror for
years. Italy was as afraid of them as a mouse is of a cat ;
Holland and Sweden trembled at the very sound of their
name ; Denmark every year paid them a large sum of
money to keep them at peace ; even England preferred to
keep out of their way rather than run the risk of meeting
them on the ocean.

An unlucky ship, which found itself near the Atlantic
coast of Africa, might see at any moment an odd-looking
boat with long lateen sails, swooping down upon her from
some sheltered inlet or harbor, where she had lain at watch
for her prey. In a twinkling she would sail alongside the

vessel, grapple her, drop her long sails over the vessel's side, and a host of swarthy Moors, with bare, sharp sabres held between their teeth, belts stuck thick with knives and pistols, would come swarming over, boarding their prizes from all sides at once.

Exasperated with these pirates, the United States sent a fleet to attack them. Decatur, a young officer, steered boldly into their harbor one night; burned one of their vessels, and, before the pirates could get themselves together, sailed coolly out, and was soon beyond their reach. Many other brilliant attacks were made upon them, until the pirates began to understand they had a new sort of a foe to deal with. Peace was declared, and there was no more trouble with pirates for a time.

Another important event in Jefferson's administration was the duel between Alexander Hamilton and Aaron Burr, in which duel Hamilton was killed.

Hamilton, you remember, had been Secretary of the Treasury; Aaron Burr had been a brave soldier in the Revolutionary times, and was now Vice-president with Jefferson.

Washington had always been suspicious of Burr, even during the war; and Hamilton had always distrusted him fully. These two had been opposed to each other many times in political schemes, but never had quarreled outright.

In those days duels were common. If a man felt that he had been insulted, he would challenge his enemy to meet

him in fight. Then these two would stand face to face
and shoot at each other.

Notwithstanding that duelling was fashionable among men

DUEL BETWEEN HAMILTON AND BURR.

at this time, the death of Alexander Hamilton, a man so
well known, and so much respected, seemed to awaken the
whole country to the horror of the deed. Burr was looked
upon as no less than a murderer, and from that time he
sank in public opinion.

Finding himself now looked upon with such contempt and

anger, he left the State, and for a long time wandered about through the western part of the country.

All at once like a bomb, came the report that Aaron Burr had been detected in a plot against the government. He had been secretly plotting to invade Louisiana, seize the city of New Orleans, stir up a rebellion in these Western States, and so break up the Union.

The country was wild with excitement. Burr was arrested and tried for treason, but nothing could really be proved against him.

Whether he was guilty or innocent could not be decided from the evidence brought forward, and he was finally acquitted. But the once brilliant Aaron Burr, was from thenceforth a disgraced and ruined man ; and his name ranked next to that of Benedict Arnold in the contempt of all good patriots.

FULTON'S STEAMER.

But the greatest event of all, was the invention of the steam-boat by Robert Fulton. For a long time it had been known that Fulton was trying to make a boat that would go without oars and without sails. Of course people would not believe such a thing could be done, and I am afraid the poor man like more inventors, had to endure a great amount of ridicule. "As foolish as Fulton," or "as crazy as Fulton," were household words in those days. Many a joke did the newspapers print at his expense, many a picture did the "funny papers" of the day make of the wonderful boat.

At last the boat was ready. At a certain hour it was promised that it should start on its first trip up the Hudson River to Albany. The docks were crowded with people jeering and mocking, ready almost to mob the brave Fulton in case the boat proved a failure.

The moment arrived. "Go, go!" cried the rowdies on the docks. "Why don't you go?" "What's the matter with the boat!" "Hooray for the steamboat!"

At last the signal was given. Imagine the anxiety in the heart of Fulton! I fancy his heart almost stopped its beating as he listened for the first thud of the machinery.

But see! the piston rises! now it falls! now a splashing of the water against the pier! and the boat is certainly moving away! On, on, she went, steadily though slowly, scaring all the other vessels from her track. The people on the dock stood with eyes and mouths wide open, staring at the moving boat. Not a jeer nor a laugh; they were too surprised even to speak.

Up the river it passed, sending forth its puffs of black smoke, and bringing the people down to the river-side as it passed along. When darkness had fallen, and the boat went puffing up the river, sending out its showers of sparks, the people who had heard nothing of this wonderful invention ran to their houses in fright. Some thought it a sign from heaven; others thought it surely must be the very Evil One himself.

JEFFERSON had been elected by the Republicans; that is, by the party who hated all form and ceremony, and who were determined to have no government that was at all like a kingdom.

Jefferson was a man after their own hearts. Although he had been brought up in wealth as Washington had been, his ideas were very different. In Washington's time there had been brilliant social gatherings at the capitol, and Washington himself always rode about in his elegant family coach.

Jefferson at once put a stop to all displays at the capitol, saying that the simple living there should be a lesson to the country. It is said that when he went to the capitol to be made President, he rode on horseback, dressed in his plain every-day clothes; that he leaped from his horse, hitched it near the entrance, and walked in unattended to the hall in which he was to take the President's oath and make his speech.

Of course such a man as this made strong friends and equally strong enemies. His friends could find no language strong enough to express their admiration of him, and even his enemies could not but respect him.

As I told you in the story of the administration of John Adams, Jefferson died on the Fourth of July, 1826. Just as he was passing away, he heard the clanging of the bells. Listening for a second, he said, " This is the Fourth of July." These were the last words of this brave, steadfast soul; this man who had stood so firmly by his country in just that way which had seemed to him right.

THOMAS JEFFERSON. 1801—1809.	*Louisiana Purchase.* *War with the Pirates.* *Steam-boat.* *Duel between Hamilton and Burr.*

JEFFERSON AND RANDOLPH.

Here is an anecdote of Jefferson and Randolph, told by an old Virginia senator. :

" When I was a boy of nine or ten I often dined

with my father at Monticello. Jefferson was a lonely man, the beauty and purity of whose family relations have been only recently made known in his biography by his niece. He took great pride in Monticello. Wanting a Chinese gong for the clock tower, in order to certainly secure it, he sent by three different vessels going to China. As it happened, each vessel brought a gong, and one he sent to my father.

" I finally presented it to the Staunton fire department. When, in those troublous days, we were melting up bells into cannon, that was also sent, but was returned as too valuable a souvenir to be destroyed.

" I did not like John Randolph. He was the most spiteful of men. If he was witty, his wit always left a sting. When I was a young man I went down to Richmond. Randolph was then in the Assembly. Charles Fenton Russell, a fine, genial man, was just concluding an address, saying, ' I am sorry to have been obliged to consume so much of the time of my fellow-members.'

" ' So am I,' squeaked out Randolph, in his high, shrill voice.

" But he did not always get the best of it. Daniel Sheffey was a little Dutch shoemaker in one of the western counties, who showed such ability that some influential persons interested in him had him taught to read ; he afterwards studied law and became one of the most brilliant and prominent men in the State. He and Randolph were in Congress together.

"Randolph was intensely aristocratic, and felt no small contempt for the Dutch shoemaker.. One day in Congress, Sheffey made a fine speech, and one in which he had shown no small degree of humor.

"This was more than Randolph could bear. He got up and in the most elaborate manner began to compliment Sheffey on his convincing logic; but added, 'Let my honorable friend keep out of the field of humor, in which his powers have not fitted him to shine.'

"Quick as a flash Sheffey was on his feet. 'The honorable member is right,' he said; 'and since he never trenches on my province, I will hereafter never intrude on his.'"

"To know Sheffey's appearance is necessary to appreciate the force of his quick retort on the house, for he had a little head, an enormous paunch, little short legs, and resembled more than anything else a human frog."

JEFFERSON'S FIDDLE.

Jefferson's fiddle was, I fancy, as dear to him as Robinson Crusoe's man Friday. At any rate it was well understood among the members of his household that any lack of care, any neglect or carelessness towards his precious fiddle could not easily be atoned for.

He used often to say, in joking his wife, as he so enjoyed doing, "It was the fiddle that won the 'Widow Skelton.'"

The Widow Skelton was quite a belle in Virginia society, and had, as the stories say, "throngs of admirers."

One day, two of her suitors, bent on learning their fate from her own lips, met in the hall of her house.

The sound of music caused them to listen. The widow was playing on the harpsichord and singing a love-song, while Jefferson accompanied her with voice and violin.

Something in the song, and in the manner of her singing, showed them that they might as well go away. So quietly leaving the hall, they mounted their horses and rode away, sadder but wiser men. In a week or two, the engagement of Mrs. Martha Skelton to Thomas Jefferson was among the rumors of the day.

Jefferson was always fond of the violin. When his paternal home was burned he asked, "Are all the books destroyed?"

"Yes, massa, dey is, but we saved de fiddle." answered the old family servant, who knew his master's pet vanity.

PRESIDENT MADISON.

THE ADMINISTRATION OF JAMES MADISON.

The next President was James Madison. He, too, was chosen by the Republicans. He had been a near and dear friend of Jefferson, and in simplicity of manners and living was very like him. He was usually dressed in a plain suit of black broadcloth, and was always very quiet and gentlemanly in his bearing. The wearing of gay colors had very much gone out of fashion since the days of Washington and Adams, and so they were not very often worn, either at the capitol or elsewhere.

When Madison became president, affairs were very prosperous and quiet. There was a prospect of trouble ahead, however, both from the Indians and from the English.

The Indians had been very quiet since the time of Washington, when Anthony Wayne had attacked them so furiously ; but now there had arisen among them a young chief, Tecumseh, who was wise enough to see that the Indians were being pushed farther and farther from their "happy hunting grounds," and that unless the white man could be driven away, they would some time have no hunting-grounds at all. And so when Harrison, the Governor of Indiana, bought from some of the chiefs a piece of land, and was about to take possession of it, this chief felt that the time had come to speak ; and accordingly the Flying Tiger, as he was called, came to Harrison about it.

" I wish to talk with you," said Tecumseh.

"Very well," said Harrison, " will you come into my house ? "

"No," said Tecumseh ; " the air of the white man's wigwam stifles me. I will talk outside."

As Tecumseh and his warriors, and Harrison and his officers gathered, one of the officers said, " Tecumseh, sit down beside your father," pointing to Harrison.

"My father ! " cried the chief, contemptuously. " The Sun is my Father ! "

Tecumseh then went on to explain that the Indian was

being driven every year farther west, that the broad lands of the country were theirs, and that no Indian had any right to sell, nor a white man any right to buy the land.

Governor Harrison tried to explain, but Tecumseh would not understand; and although he went away quietly enough, Harrison well knew that an outbreak might at any time be expected.

Tecumseh's great plan now, was to unite all the Indian tribes in one body, and so make a fearful attack upon the white men. And for this purpose he left his tribe in the care of his brother, "The Big Prophet," and travelled about from tribe to tribe, telling his story and urging them to fight against these "pale-faces," as he called the white men. If Tecumseh had succeeded in his plan, I fear it would have been a sad, sad day for those states bordering upon the Indian camps. But while Tecumseh was away, Harrison attacked the Indian camp on the Tippecanoe river, broke up their town, and drove the tribe into the forests beyond.

Tecumseh on his return, finding his own tribe broken up, and knowing that now his plan was hopeless, vowed vengeance on the Americans. Knowing that America was just on the verge of another war with England, he again journeyed from tribe to tribe, telling them what had been done during his absence, and urging them to join the English against the Americans.

Having inflamed all the Indians who would listen to him

with his own desire for revenge, he hastened to the British officers and offered himself and his warriors to fight against the Americans.

Satisfied that revenge was sure, Tecumseh and his followers were quiet during the winter months — quiet, but not idle, as the Americans learned to their sorrow a few months later.

" Dolly Madison."

Mrs. Madison was one of the most popular women of the White House. It was well indeed that her's was a heart open to social life, and that she had that warmth of heart and that brilliancy and ready wit that made her so popular and gave such charm to the White House hospitality during that administration, for Madison was, though filling nobly his political position, cold, snarling, hardly courteous in his social life.

" Dolly " was of very common " extraction," as we say, her father being a simple Quaker.

Madison was forty-three years old when he carried the brilliant, simple-hearted Dolly to the White House.

In " Presidents of the United States," John Frost, L.L.D.,

gives the following account of this kind-hearted and much loved lady :

"At Richmond, I first saw Mrs. Madison, and the instant my eye fell on her I felt that I was looking on a *Queen*. A queen she was; one of nature's queens : — she looked the character; her person, carriage, manners, language, would have been in place in any of the most polished Courts of Europe. She was large and dignified, yet she moved with easy grace. Her's was a face that seemed to bid you welcome, and to ask, ' what can I do for *y*ou?' Having once seen her, I could credit what had frequently been told me, that her husband owed much of the success of his administration (so far as his popularity was concerned,) to the influence of his wife. Her power over him was great, and all who sought favors of any kind, addressed themselves, naturally, to her, as the readiest and surest channel of access to the President. Madison was cold and shy, and a timid suitor would often have met, not with repulse, but with a polite refusal ; but Mrs. Madison anybody could approach, and if his request was reasonable he might count upon at least her good offices.

"Another beautiful trait in her character was her fondness for the young. No one could have seen her in company with young ladies, and fail to be struck with this pecularity. It became the more remarkable as she advanced in years. — At an age when to most of those who reach it the liveliness and chatter of young people is a burden, she had still the same fondness for their company; nor was there a kinder lady to be found in introducing and encouraging bashful young girls just entering society. She gained their confidence at once, and in a large mixed company, you would always find a group of youthful faces around her, all whose pleasures seemed to be her own.

"In almost every picture of Mrs. Madison she is drawn with a turban; and very properly; for it was, I believe, her constant head dress.

However the fashions might change, and however, in other respects, she conformed to them, she still retained this peculiarity. It became her well, nor could she, probably, have laid it aside for anything that would have set off her features to better advantage. So much was the eye accustomed to see it that it became, in fact, a part of her figure. It was to her much what Frederick's three cornered hat was to him. The Prussian army would have been very much surprised to see their king without his hat; but no more so than would have been the people of those days to find Mrs. Madison without her turban."

The War of 1812.

"Taxation without representation" was the cause of the American Revolution. A long phrase for little folks to remember, but easy enough after you understand what it means.

I shall have to ask you to remember a longer phrase, but I will try to explain it to you so that it will be as easy as that giving the cause of the Revolution.

The cause of this second war with England, was "*the impressment of American sailors and the capturing of our vessels.*"

Now let us see if we can understand what "*impressment of American sailors*" means.

Of course, England did not feel very kindly towards the American colonies after the Revolution. Not only had she met with a most humiliating defeat from those whom she had laughed at and called barnyard soldiers, clod-hopper militia, and many other such contemptuous names, but she had also lost a very valuable colony, one that would have been a source of great wealth to her as it grew in numbers and in power.

Ever since the Constitution had been formed, and the American Nation had seemed so full of success, England had been doing everything possible to injure American commerce. England had for a long, long time called herself the "Mistress of the Sea," and had prided herself on having the finest navy in the world.

The United States, dreading to go to war again, had borne many an insult both from England and from France.

But when the English began *impressing* our sailors, — that was a little more than we could endure.

IMPRESSMENT OF AMERICAN SAILORS.

It had long been the custom in England to fill up their ship's crews by "impressment," as they called it. This is the way they went about it. When they could not find enough men who were willing to become sailors, a party of rough men, called the "press-gang," would go upon land, look about for hearty, strong-looking young men, and, when they had found one who seemed likely to make a good sailor, would seize upon him, bind him, and carry him off to a ship.

Sometimes they did not seize upon these men, but would invite one to drink with them; and then when they had made him drunk, would carry him off to their vessel, throw him into the hold and leave him there until he became sober. Many a poor lad has awakened from his stupor to find himself on shipboard, away from home and friends, bound on a voyage which was, perhaps, to last for years. If he refused to work, he was whipped until he cried for mercy. The "press-gang" was indeed the terror of all Europe. You see now what *impressment of sailors* means; just simply this: stealing them and forcing them to become sailors on English ships.

And now, when I tell you that thousands of Americans had been seized in just this way by these English ships, do you wonder that again America declared war against England?

It was just at the close of Jefferson's Administration that an event occurred that aroused the Americans to act at once.

As the Chesapeake, one of our vessels, was crossing the ocean, it was ordered by the Leopard, an English vessel, to stop.

"I order you to stand and be searched," said the English officer.

"What do you expect to find?" asked Captain Barron.

"I search for English sailors," was the reply.

"We have no English sailors on board, and we shall not stop," answered our captain.

"You are all Englishmen, and in the name of the English government, I demand that you be searched." Immediately the English ship fired upon the Chesapeake, killing and wounding several of the crew. Three sailors were taken from the vessel and forced to serve as slaves. Such outrages as this were enough to stir the anger of any nation; and if ever war was right, it was right in such a time as this.

But in spite of all this the Federalists were opposed to war with England. They declared that if war with England were entered into, the United States would surely fall into the power of France, who was still at war with England.

It was just here that Henry Clay and John C. Calhoun, two of the greatest statesmen that America ever had, came into notice. Henry Clay was the leader of the Federalists, and was opposed to the war; John C. Calhoun was the leader of the Republicans, and was in favor of war.

Thus matters stood, when, in June 1812, Congress declared war with England.

Great was the joy in the hearts of these impressed sailors on the English ships. Many of them at once refused to pull another rope on board a ship belonging to a nation at war with their own country.

"Will you do your duty on this ship?" asked one captain of an American who was suffering under the lash for refusal to work the ship. "Yes sir," answered the man, with his back bleeding at every pore. "It is my duty to blow up this ship, an enemy to my country, and if I get a chance I'll do it."

The captain looked round in astonishment. "I think this man must be an American," he said. "No English sailor would talk like that. He is probably crazy, and you may untie him and let him go."

Over twenty-five hundred Americans who had been impressed and who thus refused to serve, were sent to prison in England, where they were kept in most wretched imprisonment until the war closed.

Many of the men were flogged — some of them till they dropped dead — but they showed the same brave spirit that they had shown years before in the Revolution. One would suppose that after being so completely defeated by the American *colonies* England would hardly have cared to go to war with the American *States*.

Hull's Surrender of Detroit.

"What!" cried the Federalists; "fight with the English on the *sea!* Expect this new weak navy of ours to fight with the great ships of England! It is madness!"

"Just wait," said the Republicans. "Just wait," said the

seamen, who were burning to avenge the wrongs of their
fellow sailors.   They did wait, and they did see.

"We shall soon conquer them this time," said the English.   "The Indians will keep up an attack on them on the
western border, and we, with our great fleets, will attack
them along the Atlantic, along the gulf, and along the
lakes on the north.   Very likely we shall gain back all
that we lost in the Revolution," said they.

And so the fighting began on the Canada border.   Gen.
Hull was in command of a fort there.   And although he
had a small garrison, still there is no doubt he might
have defended the fort and have saved it from the
English.

Brock, the English commander, approached the fort and
demanded that it be surrendered at once.   "If you don't
surrender," said he, "I'll let the Indians loose upon you,
and you know what Indian warfare is."

Unfortunately, Hull *did* know too well what Indian warfare was, and his fear of the tomahawk evidently overcame
his fear of disgrace ; for, without consulting his officers, he
hung out the white flag of surrender, and the fort with all
its provisions fell into the hands of the enemy.

His soldiers and his officers, who were ready and eager
to fight, were angry and mortified that they had been sold
so meanly.   One man, it is said, broke his sword in pieces,
and tearing his gilt lace from his coat, trampled them under

foot, saying, "We have been made to disgrace our uniform by surrendering in this cowardly fashion, without one blow."

Hull was tried for treason; but no proof could be brought against him, and he was acquitted of that charge. He was, however, sentenced to death for cowardice.

He claimed to have surrendered the fort to save his men from the horrors of Indian slaughter. Perhaps it was so; but most people believed that he could very easily have kept back both Indians and English had he tried. Hull was pardoned by the President, and lived ever after in the quiet of his home.

The American Army of Two.

During the war of 1812, there lived in a little seaport town of Massachusetts a child named Rebecca Bates. Rebecca's father was the lighthouse-keeper, and he with his family lived in a little white cottage on a point of land jutting out into the bay. This little cottage, which stood just behind the tall lighthouse, had been Rebecca's home ever since she was born.

One day Rebecca and a little girl friend of hers were sitting on the point looking off across the sunny water, when they noticed afar off, a ship apparently making in for the harbor. There was something about this ship which, though so far away, struck terror to these girls' hearts; for these were very trying days — these days of 1812 — when the British war ships could be seen bearing down upon the little sea-ports, and unloading their British soldiers to march in upon the people.

For an hour or two this ship tacked, and stood off to sea, and tacked again, and finally anchored at the mouth of the harbor. The people watching from the shore could see the boats being lowered, and the soldiers preparing to land.

Rebecca and her friend had hastened up into the tower of the light-house, and eagerly watched the movements of the soldiers in their glittering armor and gay red coats.

"O, if I were only a man!" cried Rebecca, as she thought that before night her little home might lie in ashes, burned by these cruel British soldiers.

"What would you do?" asked her friend; "see how many soldiers there are, and how many guns they have."

"I don't care," cried the hot-headed Rebecca. "I'd fight 'em — I'd use father's old gun — I'd — "

"I wonder if there will be a fight?" broke in Sarah.

"I don't know — the men in the village will do all they can."

"But see how quiet it is! not a man to be seen on the shore!"

"O, but they are hiding till the soldiers get close to land, then we shall hear the shot and the drum! O, but the drum! the drum! it's here in the light-house. Father brought it here only yesterday to be mended!"

"O, dear! what shall we do?" cried the excited Rebecca. "And see! they have reached that little sloop and are going to burn her! O, how mean! It's a shame! Where's that drum? I have a mind to go and beat it!"

"What good would that do?"

"It might scare them if nothing more."

"They would see it is only two girls, and would go on burning just the same."

"No; we could hide behind the sand-hills and bushes. Come let's go!"

"O, look! look! the sloop's on fire!"

"There! I won't stay one minute longer and see those cowardly British burn our boats! The cowards! why don't they go up into the village and fight like men? Come, let's get the drum. It will do no harm at any rate."

"All right," said Sarah, now thoroughly aroused. "There's the fife too! I'll get that."

And away the two girls ran down to the cottage for the fife and the drum; and away they scrambled among the rocks, behind the bushes and the sand hills, out towards the end of the point.

"Drum! drum! drum! Squeak! squeak! squeak!"

The soldiers out at the harbor mouth stopped their unloading, and listened.

"Drum! drum! drum! Squeak! squeak! squeak!"

"What does that mean?" asked a British soldier.

"Troops! troops!" cried another. "Troops are formed and are marching down to hem us in from the point. Hark! isn't the drum advancing?"

"Drum! drum! drum! Squeak! squeak squeak!"

"They're coming to the point surely!"

"We'd better get outside the point before we are hemmed in completely," cried another. And then the commanding officer gave the order to regain the ship.

Scrabble, scrabble! Up over the sides of the vessel like frightened rats went the red-coated soldiers, who a minute before had stepped forth so bravely into the boats intent upon subduing the simple village folk.

It took very little time for the ship to be turned about; and by the time the "American Army of Two" had reached the point, the great ship was speeding away, looking for all the world as if it had but one idea — that of getting away as soon as possible.

Rebecca and Sarah had all the time kept one eye out towards the ship, and when they saw the effect their drum, drum, drum, and their squeak, squeak, squeak had upon the mighty enemy, they could scarcely keep their time, so convulsed were they with laughter.

The people in the village meantime had been as much filled with surprise as had the British soldiers.

" What can it be?" said one.

" It must be troops from Boston," said another.

" And just in time to save us," said a third.

Then after the ship had sailed away, down rushed the villagers to the point to see the Boston troops.

Imagine their surprise to see, sitting comfortably on the rocks, their drum and fife by their side, these two girls, Rebecca and Sarah.

You perhaps can imagine what the villagers said and what the girls said; how the story of this " American Army of Two," as they were ever after called, spread through the villages and towns, and how these two girls were honored and looked upon as the preservers of their little town by the village folk.

Sarah and Rebecca grew up to be good, noble women, and when, only a few years ago, Rebecca died, her story was told all over again by the newspapers of our country, and in many a school and church honorable notice was given the good old lady, who as a child had done so much for her little town on the sea-coast of Massachusetts.

The Constitution and the Guerriere.

About a fortnight before the unfortunate surrender of General Hull, his nephew, Captain Isaac Hull, set sail from

Boston Harbor, in a vessel called the Constitution. This little vessel, which afterward became so famous, carried fifty-four guns, and was manned by as brave a body of men as we have ever read about in the history of the country.

They sailed up to the Gulf of St. Lawrence, where they cruised about for several days, watching for English vessels. One evening, at about six o'clock, the English frigate Guerriere was seen not far away, making signs to the American vessel to come and fight.

"We are quite as ready to come as they are to have us,' said Captain Hull; and he at once ordered his men to·put on full sail, and go to meet the Guerriere.

"I wonder what vessel that is. " said the English Captain; "It can not be an American ship, I am sure."

"I am sure she shows the American flag," answered an officer, who was watching her through a glass.

"It can't be," said the captain; " no American vessel would dare approach so boldly. See! she is coming as fast as she can — under full sail."

In a few minutes, however, all doubts were settled. The Constitution drew nearer, until the stars and stripes were plainly to be seen.

"What daring!" cried the English crew; and at once the Guerriere opened upon the approaching vessel a terrible volley.

Not a gun was discharged from the American vessel.

Another broadside from the Guerriere! Hull's officers began to mutter among themselves. "Why may we not return the fire?" said they.

"Not yet," answered Hill firmly. "But one man has already been killed by the British fire," said one of the crew. "Is it not time to fire, then?" said another.

"Not quite yet," returned Hull, watching the British boat, and pacing up and down the deck in great excitement.

Nearer and nearer drew the vessels, until they stood almost side by side.

"Now! fire!" commanded Hull. Bang! bang! bang! went the guns, sending such a deadly storm of fire that the Guerriere was nearly swept clear of officers and men. Rivers of blood poured over the deck in the track of this terrible fire.

Never was battle more terrible! Both ships seemed wrapped in flame and smoke; and when the smoke had cleared away, there lay the Guerriere, her masts broken, her sides torn with balls — a mere useless hulk, already sinking into the sea.

The "Constitution" now drew near, cut down the English flag, unfurled the stars and stripes in its place, took prisoner the few remaining officers and crew, and then set fire to the wreck.

Such was the battle between the Constitution and the Guerriere! a brave, daring attack on the part of Hull and his men, we know — and a brave resistence on the part of the English ship. But what can compensate for such a bloody ghastly contest !

OLD IRONSIDES.

[The following lines were called forth by a rumor that the frigate Constitution was about to be broken up as unfit for service.]

1. Ay, tear her tattered ensign down !
   Long has it waved on high,
And many an eye has danced to see
   That banner in the sky :
Beneath it rung the battle-shout,
   And burst the cannon's roar ;
The meteor of the ocean-air
   Shall sweep the clouds no more.

2. Her deck, once red with heroes' blood,
   Where knelt the vanquished foe,
When winds were hurrying o'er the flood,
   And waves were white below,
No more shall feel the victor's tread,
   Or know the conquered knee ;
The harpies of the shore shall pluck
   The eagle of the sea.

3. Oh, better that her shattered hulk
    Should sink beneath the wave ;
Her thunders shook the mighty deep,
    And there should be her grave.
Nail to the mast her holy flag,
    Set every threadbare sail,
And give her to the god of storms —
    The lightning and the gale.

                  — O. W. HOLMES.

THE WASP AND THE FROLIC.

Between ships with such lively names as these, we might well expect a lively battle.

One Sunday morning, just after sunrise, an American vessel, the Wasp fell in with the Frolic, a vessel which was guarding some merchant vessels on their way from the West Indies.

The Wasp began at once to get herself ready for a real wasp fight. The Frolic did the same ; but as she had only just weathered a severe storm, I fear she did not feel in a very frolicsome mood.

It was a rough morning. The sea rolled, the waves piled up and broke over the vessels' sides, making even the oldest sea-dogs stagger about, as they prepared for battle.

At last the signal was given, and bang ! bang ! bang !

bang! bang! bang! went the guns from both the Wasp and the Frolic. For a time it was uncertain which would stand the storm of fire.

At the very first volley the Wasp lost mast and rigging and pitched wildly about on the foaming sea, tossing her men in every direction over the slippery deck.

But, swinging round, she quickly brought her side over against the bows of the Frolic, and let fire a volley which raked the other vessel from stem to stern, carrying death to nearly every soul on deck.

And now, so close were they, that the crew of the Wasp, with yells and howls, swarmed over the sides of their vessel, boarding the Frolic with wild cheers of triumph.

Two other naval battles took place during this year of 1812, in both of which the Americans were victorious.

The English were struck dumb with amazement; and I suspect the Americans themselves were hardly less surprised. The English newspapers growled and snarled. " What ! " said they; "shall an English man-of-war, which has not been beaten since the days of Queen Elizabeth, be beaten now by a parcel of American-built ships, manned by raw sailors! Shall our Britannia, which so long has ruled the sea, be beaten by this upstart nation ! "

But notwithstanding all that *had been*, it *now was* that the American nation had proved itself as brave on sea as on land; and the great English navy was forced to acknowledge a rival.

The Lost War-Sloop.

("THE WASP," 1814.)

O, the pride of Portsmouth water,
Toast of every brimming beaker, —
Eighteen hundred and fourteen on land and sea —
Was the " Wasp," the gallant war-sloop,
Built of oaks Kearsarge had guarded,
Pines of Maine to lift her colors high and free !
Every timber scorning cowards :
Every port alert for foemen
From the masthead seen on weather-side or lee ; —
With eleven guns to starboard,
And eleven guns to larboard,
All for glory on a morn of May sailed she.

British ships were in the offing ;
Swift and light she sped between them, —
Well her daring crew knew shoal and wind and tide :
They had come from Portsmouth river,
Sea-girt Marblehead and Salem,
Bays and islands where the fisher-folk abide ;
Come for love of home and country,
Come with wrongs that cried for vengeance, —
Every man among them brave and true and tried.
"Hearts of oak " are British seamen?
Hearts of fire were these their kindred,
Flaming till the haughty foe should be descried !

From the mountains, from the prairies
Blew the west winds glad to waft her ; —
Ah, what goodly ships before her guns went down !
Ships with wealth of London laden,
Ships with treasures of the Indies,
Till her name brought fear to British wharf and town :
Till the war-sloops " Reindeer," " Avon,"
To her valor struck their colors,
Making coast and ocean ring with her renown ;
While her captain cried exultant,
" Britain, to the bold Republic,
Of the empire of the seas shall yield the crown ! "

Oh, the woeful, woeful ending
Of the pride of Portsmouth's water !
Never more to harbor or to shore came she ?
Springs returned but brought no tidings ;
Mothers, maidens broken-hearted
Wept the gallant lads that sailed away in glee.
Did the bolts of heaven blast her ?
Did the hurricanes o'erwhelm her
With her starry banner and her tall masts three ?
Was a pirate fleet her captor ?
Did she drift to polar oceans ?
Who shall tell the awful secret of the sea ?

Who shall tell ? yet many a sailor
In his watch at dawn or midnight,

When the wind is wildest and the black waves moan,
Sees a staunch three-master looming ;
Hears the hurried call to quarters,
The drum's quick beat and the bugle fiercely blown ;—
Then the cannon's direful thunder
Echoes far along the billows ;
Then the victor's shout for the foe overthrown ; —
And the watcher knows the phantom
Is the " Wasp," the gallant war-sloop,
Still a rover of the seas and glory's own !

— EDNA DEAN PROCTOR.

"DON'T GIVE UP THE SHIP."

This has come to be so much a watchword among our people, that it would never do for us to pass on without learning what it means. You have already learned the meaning of "Taxation without Representation," "Millions for defense, but not one cent for tribute." You will recall, too, that battle in the Revolution where "Molly Stark" was the watchword ; then there was the attack by Ethan Allen on the fort—when he cried, "In the name of the Great Jehovah and the Continental Congress I command you to surrender."

All these sayings uttered at one time or another by some

loyal son of America, have been passed down in our history, until they have come to be *immortal*, that is, never-dying sayings.

And now let us see how it was that " Don't give up the Ship !" came to be another of these " immortal sayings."

There was in our navy, a ship called the *Hornet* —a twin, perhaps, to the fiery *Wasp* that you have just heard about. This *Hornet*, with Captain Lawrence as its commander, was buzzing about in pretty nearly the same part of the ocean in which we found the Wasp — on the lookout for some unlucky English vessel into which to fix its stings. Soon up came the English Peacock, — strutting along, I imagine, under full sail, feeling as vain and sure of success as a real peacock might have felt when about to attack so small a thing as a hornet. But size isn't everything ; as we have already found in many a battle in the history of our country.

The *Peacock* gave the signal for battle. Instantly the furious little *Hornet* flew at the *Peacock*, and an angrier little hornet, with hotter stings, you never saw.

Boom ! boom ! boom ! buzz ! buzz ! buzz ! hiss ! hiss ! hiss ! went the fire from both Peacock and Hornet. So fast and so thick flew the balls, so hot and so terrible was the battle, that in fifteen minutes the proud Peacock had lost all her glory and her pride, all her beauty and her courage, and lay upon the waters a complete wreck.

Her hold was now half full of water ; and, knowing that

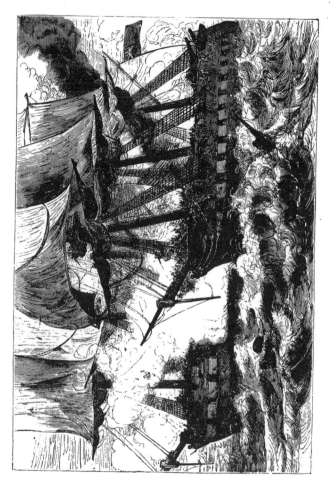

FIGHT BETWEEN THE "CHESAPEAKE" AND SHANNON."

she must sink, her commander surrendered to Lawrence, the crew were taken prisoners and transferred to the Hornet.

The generous way in which Lawrence treated his prisoners won the hearts of the British even; and his bravery carried delight to the hearts of his countrymen.

When he came into Boston harbor with the Hornet, he was greeted with shouts and hurrahs; and another vessel was given him, while the Hornet was set aside for repairs.

Now, this new vessel which was given into the charge of Captain Lawrence, had been, from its very beginning, an unlucky vessel. So much so, indeed, that the sailors were afraid to board her, believing that she was fated, and must surely bring only sorrow to her crew.

But brave Captain Lawrence willingly took command of her; feeling confident and secure after his recent victory.

No sooner was he ready to sail forth from Boston Harbor, than he met in battle the Shannon, an English vessel. I wish I could tell you that the gallant Lawrence again came out victorious. But, instead, I shall have to tell you that after a hot, fierce battle of only fifteen minutes—a battle as fierce, and hot, and terrible as had been that between the Wasp and the Frolic, or between the Hornet and the Peacock — the unlucky vessel was reduced to a mere wreck. At the very beginning of the fight, Lawrence himself, who always stood in the very thickest of the fire, fell mortally wounded.

Thus folded in his country's flag, Lawrence was carried by the British to Halifax, where he was buried with the respect and honor which he had so richly deserved.

Very carefully did his officers carry below their much loved commander; and Lawrence, not forgetting his charge even in dying, whispered almost with his last breath, " Don't give up the ship ! "

The British, wild with delight, that at last, after so many defeats, victory was once more on their side, swarmed upon the deck of the American vessel, singing and shouting with joy.

But when they found the brave Lawrence lying dead, they did not forget how nobly and how kindly he had dealt with the English prisoners at his victory over the English Peacock. And so, seizing the American flag, which they had torn from the mast with such yells of delight, they carefully lifted the unfortunate commander, and wrapped around him this banner which he had so loved, and for which he had so bravely fought.

The Friendly Foes.

Just before the " Wasp " set out on her cruise an American commodore, named Rogers, put to sea with a number of ships. One of these named the " United States " and in charge of the famous Captain Stephen Decatur, started off alone across the Atlantic to the southeast.

The " United States " was beautifully fitted up, and captain and lieutenant had spared no pains in training her crew, that she might be the most strongly manned of any vessel in the United States service.

As the vessel drew near Maderia report came of a strange vessel sighted to the southward

" If it is an English frigate, we know what that means for us," said the crew, filled with excitement.

How intently the approaching vessel was watched ! It comes nearer now — almost, almost,— yes,— now her banners can be seen. Yes, it is an English vessel. A little nearer and her name ! M-a-c-e-d-o-n-i-a-n !

" The ' Macedonian ' ! " cried the commander. " Do you say it is the ' Macedonian '? Are you sure it is the ' Macedonian '?"

"Aye, aye, sir," replied the mate ; "and a fine frigate she is said to be — as fine a one as sails the English waters."

" The ' Macedonian,' " said the commander, a troubled look creeping into his eyes. " I would rather it had been 'any English vessel than that," said he, half to himself, looking sadly out across the water at the approaching vessel.

Now it had happened that in times of peace, Decatur, our American commander, cruising around in his frigate, had often come across this frigate "Macedonian," and the two captains had grown to be warm friends. Often they had said, "What should we do if some time our frigates should meet as foes?" And always Decatur had said, "Let us not think of such a thing; for it is sure to go hard with any English foe my frigate might encounter; for I would fight, fight to the last man. No enemy should haul down her colors as long as I had left a hulk to raise them from!"

And now here were these two warm friends face to face in deadly battle. America and England were at war.

" Be ready, every man at his gun!" sternly commanded Decatur.

Nearer and nearer drew the " Macedonian." Now she is in range. The command is given; and out blaze the guns. Such a volley! The United States frigate was wrapped in smoke. The English frigate was raked from stem to stern.

" She is on fire! She is on fire!" shouted the British crew.

But she was not on fire. Another volley — another — another!

Down went one mast. "That volley made a brig* of
her!" said Decatur. "Another, boys, and she'll be a
sloop!"

How the "Macedonian" creaked and rolled! Down came
her great mizzen mast—then the "Macedonian" surrendered.
Poor "Macedonian"! Masts all broken, her sides full of
holes — what else was there for the brave vessel to do?

Now all was quiet. The firing ceased. The smoke
cleared away — there lay the brave "Macedonian," a poor,
broken wreck.

Captain Carden, the commander, the friend of Decatur
came on board the United States frigate, and, as is the
custom, stood before Decatur, surrendering his sword.

It was a hard, bitter moment for both men. Little
joy was there to Decatur in a victory that defeated and
ruined his friend.

"I cannot take your sword," said he to Carden. "I
will take your hand instead."

Then the two friendly foes clasped hands. The contest, the victory, and the defeat made a strange experience
to them. England said "Another frigate lost!" America
said, "Hurrah! Hurrah! another victory over the British!"

* A brig has but two masts a sloop but one.

A Young Hero.

On board the "United States," and during the battle you have just read about, was a boy only ten years of age, Jack Creamer by name.

In those days very many young boys were employed on shipboard, but their names were not entered upon the muster roll of the ship until they had reached a certain age, or served a certain time.

When Jack, our young hero, saw the "Macedonian" bearing down upon the American frigate, he looked troubled, "Ho, ho! Jack," cried his comrades, "you are afraid!"

"I'm not!" cried Jack, indignantly; and he hurried away to find the captain.

"Well Jack, what's wanting now?" said the captain, as the bashful boy sidled up to him, evidently wishing, yet dreading, to make some request.

"Please, Commodore, will you put my name upon the muster roll before the battle begins?"

"Why, what for, my lad?" asked Decatur, surprised.

"So that I can draw my share of the prize money when we capture that British vessel," replied the boy, bravely.

"All right;" laughed the captain: "since you are so sure we shall have the prize money to divide."

"I am sure we shall," answered Jack, simply.

The battle came on; a quick, hot battle, as you have read. Jack was stationed on the main deck — in the thickest of the fight — as powder boy. Close to one of the great guns he stood; and to keep powder ready for this gun was his duty. Back and forth between the powder magazine and the gun he hurried, the cartridges closely hidden beneath his jacket that no spark might reach them. Overhead, among the rigging, all about him on every side, whizzed the deadly leaden balls; but Jack took little heed. To keep his gun busy, to take the British ship, was all he thought or knew.

"Well, Jack," said the captain, when the battle was over, "we *did* capture the Britisher!"

"Yes, sir; yes, sir," answered Jack, his smoky, sooty face radiant with joy. "I knew we would."

"And now," continued the captain, "if we succeed in getting the old hulk safe into port, there'll be the prize money. Would you mind telling me what you propose to do with the two hundred dollars that will be your share?"

"O sir," answered Jack. "Half of it I shall send to my mother. The other half — with that I will get me a bit of schooling."

Decatur's kind heart was touched. You may be sure

the brave boy got his " bit of schooling " and that he had ever after a warm friend in the good captain.

For many years the lad served under his friend in the navy, and in his service won many honors both through Decatur's friendly interest in him and through his own unfailing courage and his strong, ready, honest bravery.

A LUCKY SHOT.

It was a beautiful Sabbath morning in July 1812, that the " Oneida," an American vessel, lay in Sacketts' Harbor. The vessel had just come into port after a long, busy season of active warfare, and the crew, tired out, were planning for a day of real rest.

But, in the early morning, just as light began to dawn, report came, " The enemy are approaching — they have entered the harbor — they are upon us ! "

At once the alarm was spread through the little town; and down to the shore rushed the people. There at the entrance of the harbor lay five men-of-war.

" What will they do?" asked the frightened people. " What can *we* avail against such a foe in this little close harbor of ours ! "

Just then a little boat was lowered from the leader of the fleet.

" See, a messenger comes ! " called one from the " Onei· da," who was watching from his high place.

Swiftly the little boat advanced. The captain of the " Oneida " waited anxiously, but so quietly that every man around him took courage.

The little boat came alongside. " The captain of the ' Oneida ? ' " asked the man in the boat.

" I am he," answered the captain.

" This message from the captain of the fleet now stationed at the entrance to the harbor : ' Let the ' Oneida ' surrender or the town will be destroyed."

But Commodore Woolsey, the brave officer who commanded the " Oneida," knew no such word as surrender. But what could he do? He could not escape, for there lay the enemy just outside the entrance.

" We do not know the word surrender," said the Commodore.   At   once   he began giving orders for action.

The villagers threw up rough breastworks along the shore, dragged down their own great gun and set up on either side a cannon which, at some time, the plucky villagers had pulled up from the sunken hulk of an old British vessel. Commodore Woolsey, meantime, ordered his vessel to the entrance of the harbor. Then he placed her in such a way that her broadside of nine guns faced the enemy.

At eight o'clock the British man-of-war came up within range. Out pealed the great gun from the shore; but alas, it sent its volley only into the water and the enemy were by no means harmed.

"Hooray! Hooray! Hooray for the Yankee gun!" shouted the British, who had a way in this war as in the Revolution, of having their laugh in the early part of the contest — perhaps, because they so rarely had it on their side in the end.

For two hours the firing went on from the shore, from the "Oneida" and from the English vessels. In all that time no one was harmed, neither side had gained one point.

"This is child's play," said a villager, impatiently, as he loaded the great gun at which the British had shouted in scorn.

But just then a whizz-z-z, then a thud, and a great cannon ball from the British fleet rolled at the villager's feet.

"We've been playing ball with the red-coats now long enough," cried he, lifting the ball. "Now let's see if they can catch back again!" And so saying he rammed the ball down the muzzle of the long gun. "Now then, old gun!" said he, as he sent the ball whizzing out across the water.

A boom, a whiz, a crack, and the Royal George was

raked from stem to stern, and fourteen men lay wounded upon the deck.

A silence followed. There was hurrying to and fro along the vessel's decks — then — what do think? — the squadron put about, and sped out of the harbor as fast as ever it could, leaving the villagers so dumb with consternation that minutes passed before it occurred to them to rejoice in their victory.

"Hooray! Hooray! Hooray!" cried they, as the British sped away. " Hooray for the Yankee gun!"

An Adventure of the Ship President.

The " President," a Yankee frigate under Commodore Rogers, sailing into the Irish Channel, took up its position just where it could worry the British vessels going in and out and prey upon the British commerce.

" This must be stopped," said the British authorities. " That one little frigate is doing more harm and making more trouble than a whole squadron. We will send a squadron out to meet this vessel. It is weak, foolish, absurd for the English government to allow the vessel to cruise about our channels in this manner. Has the English navy no power, no authority, no dignity?"

And a squadron was sent out to meet this vessel. But no sooner did it set forth than Commodore Rogers, who someway seemed never to be caught napping, heard of its approach and put out to sea.

"We will go home," said Commodore Rogers, cheerily, "I think the British will remember us even if we do stay no longer in their waters."

It was a brisk September morning — so clear and bright. Gaily the little frigate sped before the breeze, her white canvas gleaming, her cordage creaking merrily, her prow cutting the dancing waves.

All was well. But towards evening a sail was seen. "It is a British vessel," said Rogers, scanning it closely. "I think they are following us — yes — I am sure they are."

"Quick, quick, my men," said Rogers. "Up with our British banners — on with your British uniforms, and remember *now* we are the British 'Sea Horse!'"'

"Aye, aye, sir," answered the crew, ready enough to deceive the pursuing vessel — for 'all things,' you know they say, 'are fair in love and war.'"

On came the British vessel, nearer and nearer, till at last its banner could be seen. "Welcome the 'High flyer,' be ready, my men," shouted Rogers, "H. M. S. — the Highflyer."

Nearer and nearer came the vessel — now she is alongside. " Now, my good British lieutenant," said Rogers to one of his men, " you will go on board the 'Highflyer' with this message from the commodore of this, the English ' Sea Horse' to the commodore of the English 'Highflyer.' "

With great dignity and mock gravity, the lieutenant received his orders and went on board the "Highflyer."

" I am," said he to the "Highflyer," " the bearer of this message from the commodore of the British vessel, the ' Sea Horse,' it is requested that the ship books of the ' Highflyer' be sent on board the ' Sea Horse ' for comparison and, if need be, for revision.

The commodore of the " Highflyer" received the lieutenant and his message with that courtesy always observed between officers either in the army or in the navy, and on his return to his own vessel accompanied him.

" Ah, this is a fine vessel," said the commodore of the " Highflyer" as he examined the " Sea Horse." " Indeed, you do not find such a ship as this in any outside the English navy. Ah, England is the mistress of the sea! Now those little American crafts — I boarded one once — paugh! such a vessel! And by the way, have you seen anything of that little frigate, the ' President ! ' We are to overtake her—she's made trouble enough for one frigate so

we think.   They say she put out to sea this morning.
Probably knew we were after her, so ran away, coward
that she is."   And the commodore laughed loudly at what
he considered a huge joke.

It was a joke, no doubt; for the commodore and the
officers of the "Sea Horse" laughed — yes, roared with
laughter; and the commodore of the "Highflyer" strutted
and puffed up and down the deck, filled with pride and
satisfaction at his own wit.

"By-the-by, what sort of a fish is that Rogers, the
commodore of the 'President,'" asked Rogers, a twinkle in
his eye.

"A mighty odd fish, I am told," answered the commodore of the "Highflyer."   "At any rate he proves a hard
fish to catch.   But he shall be my prisoner yet," growled
the commodore — and little mercy will he get from me.
No sir! Americans — the miserable, cowardly——"

"Hold sir! do you know on whose vessel you stand
— do you know to whom you speak?" interrupted Rogers,
his eyes flashing fire at the word *cowardly*, as applied to
his nation.   "You are this minute on board the 'President.'
I am Commodore Rogers and you are my prisoner.

"Hoist the American flag—down with the British banner!" called Rogers to his crew.

The commodore of the "Highflyer" stared, turned
pale, actually gasped.   But there was nothing to be said

— nothing to be done. The " Highflyer " was surrendered, and away sailed Rogers, a harder fish to catch than ever — at least so thought the " Highflyer " and its bragging, bustling commodore.

A Story of Sackett's Harbor.

"It is useless," said the British officers stationed in Canada, "to attempt to march across the frontier to attack the Americans. But there are the lakes — their waters are open to us as well as to them. We will sail down upon them if we cannot march down upon them."

But you may be sure the Yankees' eyes were open — Yankees are not often caught napping, especially in war time. "The lakes must be fortified," said they. "The British will be sailing down upon us if we leave the great water course free to them."

But it was no easy thing to reach these frontiers in these early days. There were no railroads, not even roads through this section of the country. The same wildness, the same density of forests that prevented the march of the British down upon the American towns, made it a discouraging if not an impossible task to carry to the lakes the necessary guns and ammunition. More t_ran that, the sailors themselves looked with scorn upon the ship life on land, as they called it. "We, who have sailed the Atlantic, do not propose to end our lives in those fish ponds," said they.

But after much hard work on the part of the government, much arguing and explaining, together with promise of larger pay to those seamen, who for their dear country's sake would thus martyr themselves, sailors were gathered together for the lake expeditions. They were a jolly crew, these sailors — a reckless, noisy crew. Sledges dashing up through the Maine, New Hampshire and Vermont woods, filled with these noisy, rollicking fellows, decked out in their red, white and blue, filling the woods with their shouts and songs were common sights in those days.

It was May, 1814, and the new frigate "Superior" lay in her dock at Sackett's Harbor. She was a trim little vessel; her builders were proud of her; her captain loved her; and the crew, even the crew, eager to see her sail out over the sparkling waters of the lake.

But her stores, her cannon, her guns, her cordage — all these were to be brought from Oswego Falls some fifty miles away. Now it would be easy enough to bring them up the Oswego River, but there were English vessels blockading the harbor — and to run an English blockade was not an easy thing to do, you may be sure.

But the stores must be brought. That was a fact. That it would be no easy matter was another fact equally plain.

But Yankees can always find a way if there is a way to be found; so finally, a captain, one who had grown up and grown old on and about the lakes, and so knew every inch of the way, was found who agreed to do the best he could, though even he hardly dared hope to reach the " Superior."

He set out with the stores and cannon. By dint of sailing the clear waters by night, and lying hidden up creeks by day, the wise and wary old captain succeeded in getting within sixteen miles of Sackett's Harbor, where the English vessels lay in blockade.

But the hardest was yet to come. How were those cannon, the stores, most of all, that enormous cable weighing ninety-six hundred pounds, to be taken across the country to the dock at Sackett's Harbor? Anyone but a " Yankee " would have given up in despair. But not so the brave captain and his faithful men. " The cannon we will load on to carts. They may sink in the marshes ; they may break down in the forests ; but we'll load them, we'll load them, my boys," said the captain.

" Aye, aye, sir ! " replied the hearty sailors.

" But the cable ; ninety-six hundred pounds of cable ! " and the captain shook his wise old head ruefully.

The sailors looked at it too, and shook their heads. There it lay, a great heap of coiled rope. No cart could bear its weight; it could not be dragged; it could not be lifted; it could not be cut.

"If it could be divided among us — cut in pieces — there are two hundred of us — we —"

"Divide it! divide it! that's just the way!" shouted one great strong sailor. "'Rah for Teddy! 'Rah for Teddy! You shall have double rations for a week for that, my lad! Come on, boys, come on!"

And seizing one end of the cable, he tugged away at it, lifted it upon his shoulder, and facing Sackett's Harbor, broke into a hearty sailor song. "Come on, boys," said he. "Put your shoulder to the cable, every man of you. Come now! Single file. Forward, march, to Sackett's Harbor!"

The two hundred jolly tars fell in at once with the plan and in this way the great cable reached its destination. What fun they had! How they laughed and shouted! How the forest rang with their sailor songs!

O, but it was heavy! Their backs ached; their shoulders grew raw and bleeding; and towards the end of the journey they were a weary, lame, exhausted file of men, indeed. But they reached the town, nevertheless, and were received with shouts of praise from the people. The shouts rang out over the harbor; the rockets blazed up above the house-tops; bands played; men shouted; the town was in a blaze of excitement; the sailors were feted and feasted, praised and honored till their very heads were turned. They were the heroes of the hour.

"What can have happened?" wondered the English squadron outside the harbor, as the shouts came out across the water, and the sky lighted·up with the glare of the rockets.

"O, some Yankee victory," said one officer, bitterly.

"Those Yankees are a plucky set," answered his companion, shaking his head and scowling.

A Story of Stonington.

It was one warm beautiful morning in August, 1814, that the people of Stonington, looking out across the water saw approaching, under full sail, a British vessel.

"She is coming straight into our little bay," said the frightened people, watching from their house-tops. "Yes, she is weighing anchor. She lowers a boat — she sends us a message—maybe a challenge.

But it was no challenge—only a message; and, still a message which the good people knew only too well, polite and civil and mild as it seemed, had all the force of a command. "We wish no harm to the people of Stonington. We only ask that they leave their town that we may occupy it."

"Leave our town! our homes! our fields! our houses!" exclaimed the people, indignant, frightened, sorrow-striken.

"The militia! call together the militia! Let us decide and decide quickly—shall we leave our town or defend it?"

"Defend it!" shouted the militia, "and if need be, perish with it." And word was sent to the commodore — "the people of Stonington will defend their town to the last man."

Then such a hurrying to and fro as there was. Guns were dragged forward. Every man, woman and child set to work. Soon the British opened fire. Boom, boom, boom! went the cannons. It was a sharp, hot fight. How the women and children hurried hither and thither beating out the fires that every where about the village broke forth. How the men tugged and worked at the guns. Cannon ball after cannon ball came crashing into the village—still no one is killed, no home has been destroyed.

But see! the British have ceased firing! "It is not worth the lead," said the commodore, scornfully—and away he sailed out of the harbor. "Those Americans are strangely plucky," thought he to himself.

"Fifteen tons of lead!" exclaimed the Stonington people next day, as they set to work to clear away their streets and repair their scorched buildings. "Fifteen tons of lead poured into our village and not one man killed!"

"Probably the Britisher wanted to lighten her cargo," said one old sailor, slyly.

"Write us a poem," said the people to their village rhymster. And here is what he wrote:

> They killed a goose, they killed a hen,
> Three hogs they wounded in a pen,
> They dashed away, and pray, what then?
> That was not taking Stonington.
>
> The shells were thrown, the rockets flew,
> But not a shell of all they threw,
> Though every house was full in view,
> Could burn a house in Stonington.

Not very classical poetry, is it? But it served to amuse the Stonington people for many a long day; and even now it stands in the old records of the town, a valued, treasured bit of history in rhyme.

Commodore Perry.

There was in the navy another brave young captain —
Oliver Perry — who had been busy building a fleet of nine
vessels to attack the British vessels which had taken possession of Lake Erie.

When these were finished, he named the one which he
himself was to command, the *Lawrence*, in honor of our
dead hero.

After the vessels were finished, it was a long time before
men could be found to man them.   General Harrison —
you haven't forgotten General Harrison and the Indian
chief, I hope — sent one hundred riflemen from Kentucky,
who, dressed in their hunting suits and deer-skin leggings,
made a very funny looking crew; and a little later, the
New England States collected from their coasts another
hundred men. These men were real sailors. They had
been in service on the Atlantic, — some of them for long,
long years.

When these sailors, some of them gray-headed old sea-
logs, as they called themselves, were gathered together, it
was found their sea-legs, of which they were so proud, and
in which the country was putting so much confidence, were
entirely unfitted for marching on land. They rolled around
like barrels, and had so little idea of military orders and

marching, that their commander declared he could do nothing with them.

Much fun did these "jolly tars" have over their attempts to behave like soldiers ; and I fancy they were not very sorry when it was decided to send them to Lake Erie in stage-coaches.

So twelve great coaches were fitted out; and with a band on top, flags and streamers flying, these merry sailors started off across the country, singing and shouting, the band playing *Yankee Doodle*, *Hail Columbia*, and all the other national airs, as they rattled through the villages.

And now that the vessels were manned, Captain Perry had only to wait for the appearance of the English fleet. Day after day he waited; at last, one bright morning, the cry of "Sail, ho!" was heard from the mast-head. The English were really approaching! Word spread from vessel to vessel, and every officer and every sailor was on the alert.

Perry watched their approach through his glass, and found that there were only six ships, while he had nine; but as they drew nearer, he found that each vessel carried sixty-three guns, while his carried only fifty-four. This convinced him that if his vessels could get close upon the English, the advantage would be upon the American side; but if he allowed an engagement to take place at a distance, the sixty-three guns could do the deadlier work.

Explaining this to his men, it was agreed to advance quickly, and save their fire till they were close upon the English fleet. Then, bringing forth a simple banner, on which were inscribed "Don't give up the ship!" Perry said, "Boys, these were the dying words of the brave Lawrence. Shall we hoist this banner upon our vessel?"

Of course the men understood his meaning at once; and "Aye, aye, sir!" rang forth over the waters, followed by cheer on cheer, until it reached the very shores, and came resounding back, awaking in the hearts of the English crew a dread of what was about to happen.

Then followed a terrible scene of death and bloodshed. For three hours the battle raged. The decks ran blood; the air was filled with fire and smoke; and amid the deafening thunder of the guns, were heard the agonizing cries of the wounded.

The men fought as never men fought before, refusing to leave their guns, in spite of wounds upon wounds. At last, the Lawrence lay a battered hulk, at the mercy of the enemy. But Perry was not dismayed. Finding his own ship now helpless, only eighteen of his hundred brave men still standing, he ordered a boat to be lowered.

"To the Niagara! to the Niagara!" cried he; and wrapping himself in the flag, he leaped into the boat, and was rowed across to the Niagara.

Above him, below him, and on either side whizzed the

English balls ! Reaching the vessel, he hastily climbed her sides, and again the terrible battle was renewed.

Bang ! bang ! went the Niagara's guns ; and in fifteen minutes the battle was over. The English ships struck their colors, and the white flag of surrender was hoisted.

Two of the English ships turned to escape, but two of the American vessels gave chase, and soon they were brought back, prisoners.

The English officers, one by one, tendered their swords to Perry ; but he generously refused to take them, and treated the prisoners throughout with such kindness that the English captain himself said, "Perry's kindness alone has earned him the name of hero."

"Remember the River Raisin."

But during this time of success on water, terrible things were happening on land. Tecumseh, the Indian chief who had sworn to have his revenge on the pale-faces, had leagued himself and his men with Proctor, a British general, and most brutal Indian slaughters had followed.

No British commander was ever more hated by the American people than this Gen. Proctor. He had taken the Indians as his allies, and had encouraged and spurred them on in their bloody work. He offered presents to the Indians for bringing to him American scalps, allowed the Indians to brutally murder Americans after a battle, even when they had surrendered and had begged for mercy.

But of all his brutal deeds, none were more brutal than the slaughter at Frenchtown, a little town upon the River Raisin.

The villagers, having heard of Gen. Hull's surrender, and knowing that · now all that part of the country was in danger, had asked that Gen. Harrison, the hero of Tippecanoe, should send troops to protect them. He had, accordingly, sent a small body of soldiers, and these were now guarding the town. Gen. Winchester, too, was marching towards the town with more troops, when he was met by Proctor himself With threats of Indian massacre with all its horrors, Proctor forced Winchester to write an order to the troops within the town, telling them to surrender to Proctor.

The troops, when Proctor appeared, bearing with him this order to surrender, very unwillingly yielded. They more than half doubted that Proctor had ever been given any such orders ; but as there seemed little else to do, they at last threw down their arms, but only on condition that if they yielded themselves up thus, their wounded men in the town should be well cared for.

Proctor promised that everything should be as they

wished, and then went away, taking with him the surrendered troops; but in less than twenty-four hours the yelling, war-painted savages rushed into the village, brandishish their tomahawks, driving the people from their homes, scalping and murdering their victims with the cruelty of demons.

When at last these savages had done their worst, had butchered all, — men, women and children, — except perhaps a few who may have escaped into the forests, then they wound up their inhuman performance by piling up the dead and wounded in the homes where they had been slain, and, setting fire to the houses, danced, and drank, and howled the night away, around these terrible funeral pyres.

Proctor declared he had known nothing of the horrible intentions of the Indians, and so was not responsible for what they had done.   Perhaps this may have been true; but these very scalps torn from the heads of the murdered villagers were carried into Proctor's camp; and, since the English general received them, and the Indians went on with the same terrible slaughter whenever opportunity came, we can but think that General Proctor was not very much displeased with the behavior of the savages.

The anger of the people all over the country was aroused, and hundreds of men hastened to join Harrison's army, eager to march against the hated Proctor and his Indians.

Now, at the time of Perry's battle, General Harrison with

eight thousand men were encamped on the shore awaiting the result. No sooner had the news of the defeat of this English fleet, which was on its way to join Proctor, reached the eager army, than Harrison marched his men on to Detroit, where Proctor with his Indians held the city.

Proctor, too, had heard of the defeat of the English; and when he learned that Harrison, with his eight thousand, was marching upon him, he set fire to the stores of powder and arms and fled up the river.

On reaching the deserted city, Harrison was joined by a thousand mounted soldiers; and without stopping to rest, all together they pushed on up the river in pursuit.

They overtook the army on the Thames river — eighty miles from the city. A more hungry, tired army never was, than this of Harrison's, after their long march; but throughout the march, when it had seemed as if some *must* fall exhausted by the wayside, the cry of "Remember the River Raisin!" had always urged them on.

After a good night's rest, in which the army slept like children, they arose refreshed and ready for battle. The mounted Kentuckians, with the war cry of "Remember the River Raisin!" made the first onset.

A hot and terrible charge they made, spurred on by the thought that their dead at Frenchtown were thus avenged.

Proctor took to flight when he saw the battle turn against him. Tecumseh, burning with rage, and the desire to avenge his tribe, fought on, face to face, amid the balls which rained about him, wounded though he was time and time again, until, exhausted, he fell dead upon the field.

Then his warriors, finding their leader killed, with great yells and howls of grief, fled wildly into the forests. And thus ended the battle of the *Thames* — a complete though terrible victory for the American side.

Our Capital Taken by the English.

For some time the British ships had been blockading our coasts, and the name of their commander had come to be a word of terror in every home along the Atlantic shore. Here, there, and everywhere, his fleet had drawn up, and landed soldiers who would march up into the quiet, harmless little villages, set them on fire, and then march coolly away.

There was in England at this time a great general, the Duke of Wellington. He had just defeated the wonderful Napoleon Bonaparte in a great battle; and, as this Napoleon had been looked upon as a most wonderful being, never to be overcome by any army living, you can imagine with what respect and awe Wellington and his army were now looked upon. A general who had conquered Napoleon

Bonaparte! Why, Franklin conquering the lightning was nothing compared with it!

And now it was reported that Wellington's army had joined the British fleet and was planning to lay waste the whole Atlantic coast. Indeed, the ships were already sailing up the Potomac. Think of it! the army that had defeated Napoleon! now marching straight to attack the capitol at Washington!

There were forty-five hundred men in all; but before they had reached the city, report said there were six, then seven, even eight thousand of them. Gen. Winder hastily got together a force of seven thousand men and some cavalry. They took their station outside the city, and awaited the approach of this dreaded foe.

Three days later, the English marched up, tired and hot, ready to drop from the intensity of the heat. O, if the Americans could only have known this, if they could have known, too, that their own number was nearly twice that of the advancing foe!

But they knew only what report had told them; and so entered into the battle with little courage or hope of success.

The English army came up to them, drawn up in line just above a bridge, over which ran the road to the Capital. One charge from these Wellington troops across the bridge, and back they fell before the volley poured forth from the American lines! Another charge, quicker, fiercer, more determined! but this time the English won the bridge.

Another and another charge, and in less than four hours, the American lines were broken, and the men fled into the forests to escape the pursuit of the enemy. By evening, the English had entered our national capital. President Madison had been all day upon the battlefield; and when he saw that the defeat of the American army was sure, he rushed back to the city to warn the people of the advancing enemy. Mrs. Madison had already gathered together all that could be easily carried away, and was herself ready to leave the city.

At night, the army came into the deserted city. I suppose they expected to find much wealth and grandeur in this capital of the nation; but when you think that only fourteen years before the city had been but dense forests, you can easily understand that the seizing of this city wasn't, after all, so very great a gain to the English, nor yet so very great a loss to the country.

When the English officers entered the White House, it is said that they found the tables spread for a dinner, just as it had been prepared for the president and his party. These Englishmen sat down with a very good appetite, probably, after their hard day's work, and ate heartily. It is said that men are apt to be much better natured after having eaten a good dinner; but I am afraid it made very little difference with these officers, for they went at once to their soldiers, and ordered them to set fire to the city ; then, fearing lest the Americans might return in numbers too strong for them, they marched back to their ships and sailed away.

Their next move was to attack Baltimore ; but by the time they had reached that city, the people had learned how small a number they had, and so had lost their fear for them. They received here a strong repulse, and retired quite crestfallen.

There is a little incident connected with this attack upon Baltimore that is of interest to you all. While the soldiers were attacking the city, the English vessels lying in the bay were bombarding Fort McHenry. Just before the firing began, Francis Scott Key, an American soldier, had gone on board an English vessel to ask the commander to release certain prisoners that had been taken at Washington.

Key was kept on board during the entire bombardment. At midnight the firing ceased. What does the silence mean ?

Have the forts surrendered, or are the English driven back ? Hour after hour the brave soldier peered through the darkness, longing to catch one glimpse of the stars and stripes, which the day before had floated so proudly over the fort. Of course, if the English had taken the fort, they would at once have torn down the flag. It was during this night of anxious watching that he composed the good old song which very likely you and your schoolmates can sing. It is not so common perhaps as " Yankee Doodle," but it has become one of our national songs ; and sometime when you hear the bands playing it on our national holidays, you will be glad to remember how it came to be written.

" Oh say, can you see, by the dawn's early light,
  What so proudly we hailed at the twilight's last gleaming,
  Whose broad stripes and bright stars, through the perilous fight,
  O'er the ramparts we watched, were so gallantly streaming ; —
  And the rockets' red glare, the bombs bursting in air,
  Gave proof through the night that our flag was still there.

Chorus.

Oh, say, does the star spangled banner yet wave
O'er the land of the free, and the home of the brave?"

The End of the War.

There were other battles upon the land and other battles upon the water in this War of 1812 ; but as battles are all the same old story of murder and bloodshed over and over again, no matter how just or how unjust the cause, I think you will by this time be glad enough to come out of this cloud of fire and smoke, and breathe once more under the clear quiet skies of peace.

THE ATTACK ON
NEW ORLEANS.

The war
ended final-
ly with the
battle of New Orleans.   The
commander of the American
forces in this battle was Gen-
eral Andrew Jackson; the same Andrew Jackson who,
in the Revolutionary times, had been knocked down for refusing to clean the boots of an English officer who had taken
him prisoner.   What he had seen and what he had suffered
in those old days had filled him with a life-long hatred of
the English; and so there were few generals in the American army better fitted to fight the English than this fiery
Andrew Jackson.

On reaching New Orleans, he went to work with a will.
He formed regiments of black men — a thing unheard of **in**

those days ; and when at last the enemy approached, he and his men, both black and white, worked like ants, piling up cotton bales, sugar barrels — anything they could lay their hands on ; until they had about them a wall which Wellington himself might well have dreaded to climb.

The battle which followed ended successfully for the Americans, and with it closed the war. There was great joy throughout the country. Messengers were sent, as at the close of the Revolution, with all the speed their horses could make, from State to State ; and everywhere the bells were rung, bonfires were built, bands played and processions marched, anything and everything was done in celebration of another victory over the English, and of another time of peace.

THE ERA OF GOOD FEELING,

Let us see. We have read of how many presidents now ? Washington, John Adams, Jefferson, and Madison. And now, after the war had closed, when the country was at peace again, and both Democrats and Republicans were so glad over having conquered the English again, that they were almost willing to be good friends with each other, there came another president — James Monroe. Because of the quiet, peaceful times, during which Monroe was president, the years of his administration have been called the "era of good feeling."

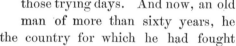

One of the pleasantest things during his administration was the visit of Lafayette to America. Lafayette was a young Frenchman who, in the war of the Revolution, had come over to our assistance in a most brave and noble way. He was much loved by Washington, and by all indeed who had known him in those trying days. And now, an old man of more than sixty years, he

PRESIDENT MONROE.

came again to see the country for which he had fought so long ago.

Everybody was glad to see him. There were the old men and women who had been in the Revolution with him, happy indeed to sit down and talk over old times with him. The younger people, too, were hardly less glad ; and so his journey from city to city, and from town to town, was one long holiday. The people of every town turned out on parades, much as did they when Washington traveled from Mt. Vernon to New York to be made president.

Everywhere he went, he was met with honor and bursts

of welcome. And it was well that it should be so. If America had in her years of success forgotten the brave Lafayette, who left his country to come to her aid when she was poor and in trouble, it would have been a disgrace indeed to us all.

When Lafayette returned home, the United States fitted out a ship to carry him. This ship they named from a certain battle of the Revolution in which Lafayette had been wounded.

I wish I could tell you that this "era of good feeling" lasted a long, long time; but, alas! I am afraid it was, as people say, only the calm before the storm; for even before Monroe's administration was quite over, there began to be serious disputes and contests upon the "slavery question."

You see the Southern people had always kept slaves, ever since that time way back in the early days of the Colonies when slaves had been brought over in the Dutch trading vessels, and had been sold to the planters. Help was needed so much in those days that colonists eagerly bought these black men from Africa to work their farms. To be sure, those Dutch traders had no more right to steal these black men and sell them than they had to steal Englishmen or Frenchmen, neither had the colonists any more right to buy them; but the colonists reasoned like this:

"They are such wild, ignorant creatures, they are really little better than my cattle. And after a little while they will be far better off here on my plantation, with plenty to eat and drink and a warm cabin to sleep in, than they were wandering about in the wilds of Africa."

This sounded reasonable, and no doubt the Southern people were honest enough and kind enough in it all, but they forgot that these black men, low and ignorant as they were, were nevertheless human beings,— and that is reason enough why no man had any right to buy and sell them.   What would you think now, children, to hear of men and women and little children being bought and sold?

As there were no State laws against slavery in those days, and even in later days, there began to be slaves here and there in all the colonies, in the North as well as in the South; but it was not very long before the States, one by one, began to make laws forbidding this selling of men and women who chanced to be black instead of white; until at last no States but the Southern now held slaves.   The Southern States held that they *must* have these black people to do their work for them, because they were so big and strong, and were used to the hot climate of the tropics.

And so this had been going on all these years; but in the time of Monroe there began to be a strong feeling that this was wrong, and that something ought to be done to put a stop to it.

And something *was* done — a most terrible something, as very likely your grandpapas and grandmammas can tell you; but I will not tell you just here about it.   I want

you first to hurry on with me over a few more administrations, and then I will tell you all about the "something"
that was done, which, in the end, freed these black men and
women and their little black boys and girls.

J. Q. Adams

When John Quincy Adams took his seat as president,
the United States were twenty-four in number.   Quite

a growth, you see, since the days of the thirteen little
States that made Washington their President.

It was during this administrationthat John Adams and
Thomas Jefferson died. I have already told you that these
two men, these life-long friends, died upon the same day.

It is said that a Fourth of July celebration was being
held in the village where Mr. Adams lived; and he had sent
to it a toast: "Independence forever." As he lay dying,
at sunset time, those who watched by his bed could hear
the distant shouting at the village, when the people heard
the old man's last message.

One more event in this administration we must speak of,
and then we will pass on to the administration of the plucky
General Jackson, the man who made it so hot for the English at New Orleans during the war of 1812. The first
railroad was laid during this administration — a little

THE FIRST TRAIN OF CARS.

road only three miles long, leading from the granite quar-
ries at Quincy, Mass., to the wharves. These cars were
drawn by horses, and I fancy it was a funny enough looking train of cars. It was not until two years later that an

engine was used.   On the previous page is a picture of the
first train of cars drawn by a real engine.

Evils of Early Rising.

I am sure you will be glad to hear that there was one
" great man" who enjoyed a morning nap as much as you
and I do ; and that he enjoyed a good joke at the expense of
a certain other " great man" who was as fond of " rising with
the lark" as the first man was of sleeping soundly.

John Quincy Adams was an enthusiastic advocate of
early rising.   He practiced it from boyhood, and attributed
to it his good health, and physical vigor in old age.   Judge
Story, who was an intimate friend, loved dearly a good
morning nap, and their opposite opinions often gave rise to
sharp and witty discussions.

On one occasion, the judge invited the ex-President to
talk to the students of his Law School, and Mr. Adams
made interesting remarks, touching, among other topics,
on his favorite theme of early rising.   The Judge then
delivered his usual lecture.

The afternoon was hot, and the lecture-room close.
Towards the close of the lecture, he noticed that the class
were nodding to each other and smiling.   Looking first on
his right hand and then on his left, he discovered the secret
of their merriment.   The distinguished visitor was asleep

and nodding ! He could not resist the temptation to add a postscript to his lecture. "Young gentlemen, I call your attention to the visible proof of the evils of early rising."

The loud laugh that followed awoke the gentleman but he did not understand the joke that caused it.

ANDREW JACKSON.

And now we come upon the next President, — a President who has been more widely popular than any other President since Washington.

We have already heard enough of this man to be able to form some idea of what his character was. Fiery, determined, as he was, hating England with all his heart, he was almost a dangerous man to put in power — except for one quality which offset all the rest ; and that was that he loved his country more, far more, than he loved his own interests, and so was sure to be true to her, let come what would.

The greatest event of this administration, which as far as wars or home troubles are concerned was very uneventful, was the introduction of the first steam-engine for railroad travelling.

Ever since the success with the steam-boat, thoughtful

PRESIDENT JACKSON.

men had been trying to invent some way of traveling on land by steam. There was the same kind of hooting and sneering and joke-cracking over this that there had been so short a time before over the steam-boat. Strange, isn't it, children, that we do not learn from past experiences like these not to sneer and scoff at every new thing that comes up from time to time.

Jackson had opportunity before his term was over to display the force of his iron will in a way that will make him forever to be remembered. First, he made an attack upon the money system of the country. I shall not try to explain it to you ; but when I tell you that he so upset the whole system that hundreds of wealthy bond-holders failed in their business, you can imagine that it was no slight disturbance. He actually forbade the putting of any more money into the National Bank, and dismissed the Secretary of the Treasury because he dared not obey his order. It was a fearful time for the country ; but Jackson carried the day, and the Democrats were delighted.

Then came up trouble over the "tariff" question. The South said, "We want free trade, and we're going to have it. If Massachusetts wants "protection," let her have it. But WE are going to have "free trade."

But Congress said, "No ; we can't make a law for one part of the United States which is not for the whole United States. Either *all* must have free trade, or *all* must have protection."

Then the South waxed hotter and hotter. They held public meetings, and these States, especially South Carolina, declared the tariff laws were "null and void" by that they meant they were useless, powerless, and that they would pay no attention to them. These Southern people were therefore called "Nullifiers." As the conflict went on, they went so far as to say they would withdraw from the *Union,* and have a government of their own, and so do what they pleased in their own States. They even began to raise an army with which to carry on the quarrel.

When news of this reached Andrew Jackson's ears you may be sure there was a blaze of wrath. "What! break up the Union!" said he. "Never! Haman's gallows were not high enough to hang the man upon who would raise his

HENRY CLAY

finger to pull down our Union." You may be sure it was not many hours before a proclamation was sent to those

"Nullifiers," ordering them back into place. An army was raised; ships were sent to guard the harbors; the forts were ordered to be on the lookout for the first sign of disobedience — in short, Jackson was ready, if that little State of South Carolina had dared make one show of rebellion, to crush her before she should have time to strike one blow. It is hardly necessary to say that under such determined action as this, the Nullifiers settled down; their public meetings were stopped; their army broke up and went quietly about its business — and there was peace again.

In the Senate, this matter was of course discussed. And just here, there came into notice three most remarkable men — men whom you must try to remember as long as you live. They were Daniel Webster, who stood staunch and firm for the Union, John C. Calhoun, who represented the Southern States and was, therefore, a hot "Nullifier," and Henry Clay, who, because he seemed always to find a way to settle the fiery disputes between these two, came to be called the " peace-maker."

After these troubles had been somewhat quieted, Jackson, or "Old Hickory," as his followers used to like to call him, was glad enough, when his second term was out, to go to his home and rest. He was getting old and was tired of office, he used to say; and when we recall what a life he had had, we can well believe that he did long for quiet in his remaining years. He was very anxious that Van Buren, his colleague in office, should be the next president; and he worked hard to secure his election. A word or two in the next chapter about "Old Hickory," and then we shall leave him, and hurry on to other Presidents.

Andrew Jackson's Nick-name.

They say that the way General Jackson came to be nick-named "Old Hickory" is as follows: — During the Creek War he had taken a severe cold, and his soldiers had made a shelter for him of hickory bark.

The next morning a tipsy soldier, not knowing what he was about, kicked at the bark shelter and over it went.

Jackson, speechless with rage, sprang out of the hickory heap and rushed towards the drunken offender.

"Why I didn't know you were in there, Old Hickory!" shouted the soldier.

For an instant a shout of laughter broke from the camp; but one soldier, quicker-witted than the others, called "Three cheers for Old Hickory."

The drunken soldier was saved a punishment, Jackson's temper was quieted, his dignity maintained—and he received a new name.

Jackson's Obstinacy.

That Jackson was very stubborn, even his closest friends admit. His stubborness, very likely, may not have added to his agreeableness as a friend and companion.

That Jackson was stubborn there is no doubt, but his stubbornness certainly rendered this country good service during his administration.

This strong, self-educated, self-respecting man had certain peculiarities of pronunciation, which he had acquired in childhood. The word *development*, for example, he would pronounce as though it were written devil-*ope*-ment.

One day, during his Presidency, he was conversing with a foreign minister. The gentleman, though not an Englishman, had been educated in England, and prided himself upon his correct pronunciation of it. "Devil-*ope*-ment," said General Jackson, thereby causing the minister to raise his eyebrows, and to pronounce the word correctly. The President, apparently not noticing the impolite correction, again said, " devil-*ope*-ment."

Again the minister repeated the word with its proper accent, saying with emphasis, " de-*vel*-opment."

"Excuse me, Mr. Dash. You may call it de-*vel*-opment if you please; but I say devil-*ope*-ment, and will say devil-*ope*-ment, as long as I revere the memory of good old Dr. Waddell!" referring to a former respected teacher.

The anecdote is a graphic illustration of two traits which marked General Jackson. He feared the face of no man, and he allowed no one to *push* him from a position he had taken. Few men so imperfectly educated as was General Jackson would have had the courage to adhere to a false pronunciation in the face of a scholar who corrected him.

Of course, an obstinate, wrong-headed man is liable to make serious blunders. But that risk is compensated for by this fact: no man accomplishes much who has not stubborn resolution, and having a high standard does not stubbornly endeavor to attain it.

General Jackson's Portrait.

If President Jackson had been allowed to have his own way we should have no picture of him to grace our historic galleries; for if there was any one thing that this obstinate man disliked, it was "picture painting."

"Never! never!" thundered he, "shall my face be set up here and there and everywhere."

"My face shall be my own," shouted he, as a fellow-politician begged him to allow his likeness to be painted. "My country has a right to my likeness, do you say?" cried he rising in fury. "I say they have *not*. My years and my service are theirs; but my face! Never!"

Few dared brave the thunder of this man, much as his likeness was desirable.

At one time the King of France sent to Andrew Jackson an artist, with the request that the French court be favored with a portrait of America's President. He found the ex-President sitting erect in his chair, surrounded by pillows, and his courteous presentation of his request and his credentials were received with flashing eyes.

"You can't paint my portrait, sir!" roared the general. "The King of France or any other man cannot have my picture!"

"But," said Mr. Healy, "I have come many thousands of miles, at great labor and expense, upon a commission from a reigning monarch who greatly admires you. Pray reconsider your refusal."

"No, sir," said Jackson, "you can't paint my portrait! You are welcome to stay at the Hermitage the rest of your days if you like, but you can't have my portrait."

The shrewd artist seized his opportunity; he remained at the Hermitage, and at last, with the assistance of the general's family, induced the obstinate old gentleman to give him short sittings.

CALHOUN AT HOME.

Although Calhoun and Webster were always bitterly opposed in political life, they did not fail to appreciate each other's talent and real honest worth. We aren't all of us always so fair as the little boy who said of a rival class-mate, "I hate Jimmie Waters 'cause he gets ahead of me; but just the same I know he's a heap smarter than I am."

To hold a fair, honest judgment of an enemy, to judge him without petty personal prejudice, is a thing that many a grown-up boy and girl fails to do.

Webster was big and broad enough to do this. While hating Calhoun as a politician and an enemy, no one more thoroughly appreciated his talent and respected his manhood than he did. On Calhoun's death it was Webster who pronounced his eulogy and gloried in the opportunity to do the dead man justice.

Webster's famous eulogy was a noble compliment; but nobler still was the love and reverence of Calhoun's own household. To remain a hero for a lifetime in one's own family, to be still respected and reverenced by those who have for years known one's daily life, is a greater proof of real nobility than any public eulogy can ever be.

The great man's family loved him even more than they admired him; and yet they exulted in his career. "Come soon again," said a younger brother to the eldest son, as he was leaving the homestead for his home in Alabama. "Come soon again and see us, for do you not see that father is growing old? and he is the dearest and best old man in the world!"

His own daughter in speaking of him, to a gentleman with whom she was conversing, said, "I wish you had known my father;" "You would have loved him. People admired him, but those who knew him in his family reverenced him. We all worshipped him."

She often went with her father to Washington during the Congressional session. Great and self-reliant as was the statesman, he took pleasure in talking with his gifted child, and often made her his confidant in perplexing cases.

"Of course," she said, referring to the high compliment he paid her, "I do not understand as he does, for I am comparatively a stranger to the world; yet he likes my opinion, and I frankly tell him my views on any subject about which he inquires of me."

His tenderness and consideration for his children was remarkable in so busy and perplexed a life as his.

A younger daughter, being an invalid, found her favorite occupation in reading. She was allowed to go to the letter-bag when it came from the office, and select the papers she wished to read. Once, two papers concerning news of importance which her father was anxious to see, were taken by her to her own room. But he would allow no one to disturb her until she had finished reading them.

Danl Webster

Our public men are often tempted to sacrifice their families to official life. If Mr. Calhoun was thus tempted, he never yielded to it. His cheerful home was more attractive to him than the Senate Chamber.

The Home of Webster

Daniel Webster loved nothing better than to get away from the noise and hurry of his political life and shut himself away in the quiet little village of Marshfield, where he could hunt and fish and farm to his heart's content.

He used sometimes to say, "I doubt if the applause of the Senate gives me half such real pleasure as my good broad acres, with all the rest they bring me."

We can usually judge a man's character by his house and lands. Some seem satisfied with a plain, staring, square box of a house, hedged in by street and block; others choose broad grand prospects, or beautiful hilly bits of woodland.

Webster's home, as we might suppose, was broad and grand; it had the hill, the plain, the woods, and the ocean.

A writer who saw it some years ago, before the house was burned in 1878, describes it as follows:

A long, stone wall, painted white, runs in front of the farm. Within, one sees a large meadow and an old, scattering orchard. It is a broad domain. Leaving the road and entering the winding drive-way, one passes under beautiful shade-trees, till at length he reaches a large, ancient-looking white house.

Near it stood a little white building, scarcely more than ten feet square. Here the famous orator spent many days in hard thought and study.

A very interesting spot is the resting-place of Webster. We pass by the house and the large barn and little lakes and ornamental trees, and walk on through field, and meadow, and orchard.

Now we come out upon a little open plateau of land covering two or three acres. There is not a tree or shrub upon it. It is native soil, unturned by any plow.

To the north, a vast marsh stretches away for several miles. To the west, more marsh, and then higher land, with timber. To the south, a level half mile of open field;—Webster's field, and then hills and woods. To the east, low, marshy land and the sound of the surf-beating ocean two miles away. There is no house near. Only the quiet or rugged aspects of nature; of broad-handed, far-reaching nature.

It is here that the gifted senator and his family rest. On the southern slope of this elevation of land a space is fenced off by an iron railing, some eight feet high.

In this inclosure lies buried the Webster family. Within this iron fence lies the wife whom Webster tenderly loved. Also Major Edward, his son, who died in the Mexican War, and Col. Fletcher, who died in 1862–3, from wounds received in his country's service. The Websters were a race of brave men.

Webster's grave is situated at the north end of the plot in this little jut of land. A mound of earth is thrown up, some four feet high, and overgrown with grass; at the head of this is a simple, pure white marble slab, some fifteen by ten inches, bearing this inscription, — "Daniel Webster."

In this obscure place reposes this man whose eloquence charmed a nation; upon whose lips ten thousand hung delighted; who walked among crowds of noble men, "the observed of all observers."

Daniel Webster's Fishing.

This great man, as we please to call him, could enjoy a quiet day of hunting and fishing, and could, moreover, appreciate fun as well as any boy you know. A friend of his relating anecdotes of this great man, once told the following:

"As I was quite an expert in trouting and shooting, Webster used always to send for me to dance attendance on him, while he was here to enjoy himself and relieve his mind from the toil and trouble of Congress.

"One day he came for me to go to Marshpee River, on a two day's trouting trip. We arrived there at night; and in the morning we were at the brook or river at eight o'clock, and pulling on his long rubber boots (he always took them when he went fishing : they were very long, and kept in position by a kind of suspenders) "we stepped into the brook and waded down stream, fishing with live bait (mummy chubs) ; he went ahead and caught all the large ones.

"I followed behind and caught what escaped his hook. I also carried a net. We had been fishing for a couple of hours with good success, when I heard him call, —

"'George, George, come here quick! I have got a mighty fellow hooked!'

"I hurried down to him, and saw his line leading under the bank. I riled up the water with mud above so that the trout could not see me, then run my net under the bank and scooped out the trout; he was a noble fellow, weighing at least three and a half pounds.

"'Ah! ah!' exclaimed Webster, 'we have him! Look at him, George; did you ever see such a big fellow?'

"'Yes,' said I, 'I have caught as big a trout as that.'

"'Confine yourself to the question,' said Mr. Webster; 'did you ever see so big a trout, George?'

"'Seen as big a one?'

"'Yes.'

"'Yes, I have seen and caught as big a trout as that.'

"Mr. Webster surveyed me as I stood there deep in the water, and said: 'Ah, George! I fear I shall never make anything of you! You are an amphibious creature. You *lie* in the water, and you *lie* out of the water. Come let's start home.'"

Van Buren.

There is very little of interest to little folks in this

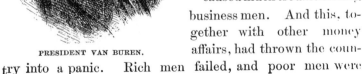

PRESIDENT VAN BUREN.

administration. You will find Van Buren very severely criticised by some; but when we think what a hard position he had to fill just after Jackson's hot-headed career, we shall wonder that he did as well as he did. All these bank changes which Jackson had made, had caused much trouble among business men. And this, together with other money affairs, had thrown the country into a panic. Rich men failed, and poor men were

without work ; provisions came to be very high, and there
was no money to buy with.   These were "hard times," indeed ; and because everybody blamed the government, they
seemed to think Van Buren was to be blamed too, though
I'm sure I don't see why he was to blame for what had
been brought about by the previous administration, or for
the ill luck of speculators and other business men.

" TIPPECANOE AND TYLER TOO."

When Van Buren's term was nearly out, his party nominated him for President again ; but the other party set up
Harrison, the hero of Tippecanoe, with John Tyler for Vice-
President, in opposition, and made the land so ring with
their song "Tippecanoe and Tyler too," that they carried
the country by storm.

It is said that this was one of the most exciting times our
country ever saw.   The Republicans had now taken on the
name Democrats, and the Federalists now called themselves
Whigs, in remembrance of the Whigs of Revolutionary
times.   Party feeling was now hot again and the campaign
was a lively one.

General Harrison had been living very quietly in a log-
cabin out in the western part of the country ever since the

war of 1812 ; and so when he was nominated for president
by the Whigs, the Democrats said, "Pshaw ! give Harrison
a cabin and a barrel of hard cider, and he'd never care
whether he became president or not." At this the Whigs
raised the cry of " Cabins and hard cider for us ! " and from
that, the campaign has ever since been called the " log cabin
and hard cider campaign." It was a hot contest ; but there
was much fun mixed up with it. The newspapers had pic-
tures of log cabins at their heads, there was " log-cabin
calico," and " log-cabin wall-paper." The women used to
meet together and make " log-cabin quilts," and the men and
boys used to roll barrels of cider through the streets.

It ended in " Tippecanoe and Tyler too " as President and
Vice-President. There can be no doubt, judging from the
bravery and wisdom of General Harrison in all that we have
heard of him, that he would have made a good president ;
but in only one month from the time he took his chair he
died, — worn out, it was said, by the excitement and hard
work of his election.

Tyler, the Vice-President, now took the chair. The great
event of his time was the invention of the telegraph system.
We have read of the invention of the steam-boat and of the
railroad, and now comes the telegraph. Of course there
were plenty of people who pooh-poohed at the idea of
" talking through a wire," but the invention succeeded
nevertheless in spite of their scoffs.

PRESIDENT TYLER,

At the same time Samuel Morse was busy inventing his telegraph here in America, another man in England, and another in Germany were busy with the same kind of work-

By and by, when Morse's telegraph had been tried between Baltimore and Washington, and had been found successful, he went to Europe to try to get it accepted there. There the three inventors, the American, the Englishman, and the German met. Of course each presented his own invention, and hoped his might be the one to be accepted by the country ; and just here you must know what a brave unselfish thing the German did. Much as he wished his own invention to be accepted, he carefully examined the machine that Morse had brought, and seeing that Morse's was really the better, he generously said, " Gentlemen, I willingly withdraw from the field ; Mr. Morse's invention is better than mine."

Wasn't this big-hearted in the German — to give up so nobly his life-work and his chance at being remembered for ages as the inventor of this wonderful machine, and to turn and frankly take the hand of his rival and wish him all success? Captain Lawrence and Oliver Perry, and all the other naval and military heroes were indeed brave men, and we admire them for their courage ; but it takes a bigger, grander soul, boys, to frankly and generously acknowledge the inferiority of one's self, than to face the cannon's roar.

A Small-Tail Movement.

In no campaign, perhaps, has there been so much rollicking "good time," so much extravagant parade and noise, so much ridiculous story-telling as in this campaign of ' 1840."

It is said that in a certain village of Western Virginia, while a speaker was setting forth in glowing colors the wonderful generalship of Harrison, a tall, angular farmer rose and called out,

"Mister! Mister! I want to ax a question!"

"I shall be happy to answer any question, if I can," replied the orator.

"We are told, fellow-citizens," said the quaint man, addressing the crowd, "that Gineral Harrison is a mighty great gineral; but I say he's one of the meanest sort of ginerals. We are told that he defended himself bravely at Fort Meigs; but I tell you that on that occasion he was guilty of the *Small-Tail Movement*, and I challenge the speaker to deny it!"

"I don't know, my friend," replied the orator, "what you mean by the 'Small-Tail Movement.'"

"I'll tell you," said the quaint man. "I've got it here in black and white. Here is 'Quinshaw's History of the United States'"— holding up the book —"and I'll read what it says: 'At this critical moment, General Harrison executed a *novel* movement!' Does the gentleman deny that statement?"

"No; go on."

"Well, he executed 'a *novel* movement.' Now here's Johnson's Dictionary,"— taking a small book out of his pocket, "and it says, 'NOVEL — *a small tale!*' This was the

kind of movement Gineral Harrison was guilty of.   Now,
I'm no soger, and don't know much of milentary tic-tacks, —
but this I do say : a man who, in the face of an enemy, is
guilty of a *Small-Tail Movement*, is not fit to be the President of the United States, and he shan't have my vote."

James K. Polk.

The next President was James K. Polk.   His administration is marked by the Mexican War — and a terrible
war it was indeed.   We do not hear so much about this
war, and do not realize how fierce a fight it was, because
the battles were all fought away off in the Mexican neigh-
borhood, and we did not therefore *see* the battles fought as
we did in the other wars.

Away back in those times when the different European
nations were all sending men over here to find lands and
gold, the Spaniards had taken possession of that part of the
country called Mexico.

Some time I want you to read about the wonderful
people the Spaniards found living there.   They had cities,
and elegant palaces and gardens ; they had a king, and a
brave king he was, too, and lived on the whole, in quite as
civilized a way as did the Spaniards themselves.   It seems

strange that these people should have been so civilized
when all the other Indians throughout the country were so
wild and savage.   It is a great mystery where these people
came from and who they were ; but as they had no written
history, it doesn't seem very likely that we shall ever find
out.   It is all very wonderful ; and when, down in this
Mexican country, and out through our Western States, we
dig up here and there axes, chisels, knives, beads, brace-
lets, even bits of cloth and pieces of vases which we know
must be hundreds and hundreds of years old, it makes us
think that this Earth of ours has rolled on and on for many,
many more years than we have any idea of.

But you will think I have forgotten all about the Mexican
war.   Mexico, as I said before, was in the possession of the
Spaniards.   Spain had never been very successful with her
American possessions, some way.   She had had, from time
to time, to give up a part of her land, once to France, and
again to the United States.   Then, too, from the very
beginning, the Spanish rulers had been very cruel and
overbearing in their treatment of the people whom they
had found in Mexico.   It is no wonder, then, that after a
time the Mexicans rose in arms, and declared they would
no longer be ruled by Spain.   Many a hot battle they had ;
but at last Spain gave up her claim upon them, and they
were independent.

There were, in that part of Mexico called Texas, many

Americans who had gone there to farm and to raise cattle. These Americans took part in the uprising of the Mexicans against Spain, and helped them to throw off the Spanish rule.

As time went on, and cattle-raising came to be a very paying business, Texas began very rapidly to fill up with these shrewd Yankees, anxious to grow rich as soon as possible.

The Mexicans at last began to grow afraid and jealous of these thrifty Yankees. "They will get our land away from us," they said. And so, when the American colony in Texas sent Stephen Austin to the Mexican government to ask that Texas should be allowed to join the Mexican Union, instead of giving him a ready answer, and sending him back to his people, they kept him for a long time in uncertainty. Austin was angry enough at this needless delay, and he wrote a letter to the Texas people telling them to rise in arms and declare themselves independant of Mexican rule. This letter fell into the hands of the Mexicans, and Austin was put in prison.

This kindled the anger of the Texans, and they rose indeed. There was much sharp fighting, and in the end Texas declared herself independant, made a government of her own and chose a governor of her own.

Very soon, she asked the United States to allow her to join *their* Union, and so be under the protection of some government greater than her own. For a long time congress talked and talked upon the matter. The Northern States said, "No, Texas is a slave-state, and we have too many slave-states already; besides we shall be sure to get into a war with Mexico, if we have anything to do in this matter." The Southern States argued in just the opposite way; but at last the State was accepted, and as the Northern States had predicted, war did follow.

I shall make no attempt to tell you much about this war — it was like all other wars a series of terrible battles in which thousands of men were killed, and thousands of homes made desolate. It ended at last in the victory of the Americans over the Mexicans, and Texas now belonged to the United States — a far dearer purchase, I think, than that of Lousiana away back in Jefferson's time.

There are a few names and incidents connected with this war which you need to know, even if you don't quite yet learn the names and stories of the battle. Certainly you must know about "Old Zack," as his men used to call him. He was a sturdy old soldier who had fought like a "Trojan," as people say, in the battle of 1812. He was very much such a man as "Old Put" had been in the Revolutionary times, and "Old Hickory" whom you heard of in that famous battle at New Orleans. And for this reason, his men had given him the pet name of "Old Zach." He did some lively work in this Mexican war, lived through it all and came out of it hale and hearty, and so much respected by the nation, that they made him President by and by.

There are several little stories told of General Taylor in this war. At one time Santa Anna, the Mexican general, sent a messenger to General Taylor. On reaching there the messenger found Taylor sitting idly on his horse, with one leg thrown over the pummel of the saddle.

"What are you waiting for?" asked the messenger, amazed at such coolness in battle.

"I am waiting for Santa Anna to surrender," replied he calmly.

At another time, some one of Taylor's officers suggested that his pet horse, "Whitney" could be too easily singled out by the enemy's shot and urged him to take another and send "Whitney" away. "Not a step," said General Taylor, "the old fellow missed the fun at the other battle but she's going to have her share in this one."

Then there was General Kearney, who had a way of marching straight into the little mud-built villages, demanding the governor of the town to present himself, and then, having surrounded him with American officers, compelled him to swear faithfulness to the United States. He would then unfurl the stars and stripes over the house of the governor, and march cooly on.

There was Captain Fremont, a noble young officer, who fully deserved his promotion to *captainship*. He had crossed the Rocky mountains at one time, had climbed one of its very highest peaks, and had there unfurled the stars and stripes. That peak, which when you come to study Geography, you will be very likely to hear about, is now

CAPTAIN FREMONT.

called *Mt. Fremont* or *Fremont's Peak*. Soon after this young officer was made captain, he started off to Oregon, passing through Mexican territory on his march. I wish I could tell you about his guide Kit Carson, who had lived for years among these wild mountain regions. Kit Carson, was a wonderful story-teller; he could tell you bear stories and Indian stories of the most exciting kind. There were hundreds of these — all out of his own life — and terrible enough some of them, to make your hair stand on end.

Toward the end of the war General Scott, who was as great a general in this war as General Taylor, was preparing to storm a place known as Grass-hopper Hill. It was a fearful place to attack, situated as it was on a rocky height, a hundred and fifty feet above the plain. A stone-wall surrounded it at the top, and within this was a military school of a hundred boys from ten to twenty years of age.

Two columns of soldiers advanced to attack the fort from either side. Slowly they toiled up the rocky steep, up to the very cannon's mouths. Pillow, the leader of one column, when half way up, fell, terribly wounded by a Mexican shell. "Carry me up with you, boys," he begged, "that I may be there to see the victory." His soldiers carried him, up amid the fire rained down upon them from the fort, and he did see a victory.

Reaching the top, quick as a flash the ladders are thrown against the walls, the men scramble over, pell mell, helter-skelter, in order and out of order, and met the Mexicans hand-to-hand. In the midst of the blood-shed, fighting as hotly as the oldest warriors, were the hundred lion-hearted boys.

" They were pretty little fellows, and they fought like little soldiers, as they were," said an American officer in speaking of them after the war.

GENERAL WINFIELD SCOTT.

It was a cruel battle ; but I am glad to say it was the last of the war. The next morning, General Scott rode into the city square, and took possesion. The Mexicans were glad enough to accept almost any terms of peace, after the battles in which they had been so terribly beaten.

It is said that after one of these terrible battles, the Mexican women gathered upon the bloody field, working througb the long, dark night, comforting and aiding the wounded and dying, both American and Mexican. Brave, tender-hearted, Mexic women ! Many a dying soldier that night had reason to thank the women of a nation he had tried so hard that day to crush.

War may seem to you a very grand thing, my boys, when you see the soldiers marching along your street, dressed in their gold and silver bands and with their plumes waving so gaily in the breeze ; but when you think of the heartache, the pain, the agony, the death that follows in every battle, no matter how grand and victorious your general may have been — then war loses its brightness and its flash ; and we have only the dark, black cloud of death to look upon.

THE ANGELS OF BUENA VISTA.

Speak and tell us, our Ximena, looking northward far away,
O'er the camp of the invaders, o'er the Mexican array,
Who is losing? who is winning? are they far or come they near?
Look abroad, and tell us, sister, whither rolls the storm we hear.

" Down the hills of Angostura still the storm of battle rolls ;
  Blood is flowing, men are dying ; God have mercy on their
      souls ! "

Who is losing? who is winning? —"Over hill and over plain,
I see but smoke of cannon clouding through the mountain rain."

Nearer came the storm and nearer, rolling fast and frightful on!
Speak, Ximena, speak and tell us, who has lost and who has
　　won!
"Alas! alas! I know not; friend and foe together fall;
O'er the dying rush the living: pray, my sisters, for them all!

　　.　　.　　.　　.　　.　　.　　.　　.　　.　　.

Dry thy tears, my poor Ximena; lay thy dear one down to rest;
Let his hands be meekly folded, lay the cross upon his breast;
Let his dirge be sung hereafter, and his funeral masses said:
To-day, thou poor bereaved one, the living ask thy aid.

Close beside her, faintly moaning, fair and young, a soldier lay,
Torn with shot and pierced with lances, bleeding slow his life
　　away:
But, as tenderly before him the lorn Ximena knelt,
She saw the Northern eagle shining on his pistol-belt.

With a stifled cry of horror straight she turned away her head;
With a sad and bitter feeling looked she back upon her dead;
But she heard the youth's low moaning, and his struggling breath
　　of pain,
And she raised the cooling water to his parching lips again.

Look forth once more, Ximena!" "Like a cloud before the wind

Rolls the battle down the mountains, leaving blood and death
    behind ;
Ah ! they plead in vain for mercy ; in the dust the wounded strive ;
Hide your faces, holy angels ! Oh, thou Christ of God, forgive ! "

Sink, O Night, among thy mountains ; let thy cool, gray shadows
    fall ;
Dying brothers, fighting demons — drop thy curtain over all !
Through the quickening winter twilight, wide apart the battle
    rolled ;
In his sheath the sabre rested, and the cannon's lips grew cold.

But the holy Mexic women still their holy task pursued,
Through that long, dark night of sorrow, worn, and faint, and
    lacking food ;
Over weak and suffering brothers with a tender care they hung,
And the dying foeman blessed them in a strange and Northern
    tongue.

Not wholly lost, O Father, is this evil world of ours ;
Upward through its blood and ashes spring afresh the Eden
    flowers.

    .   .   .   .

THE MARTYR OF MONTEREY.

The strife was stern at Monterey,
    When those high towers were lost and won ;

And, pealing through that mortal fray,
  Flash'd the strong battery's vengeful gun ;
Yet, heedless of its deadly rain,
  She stood, in toil and danger first,
To bind the bleeding soldier's vein,
  And slake the dying soldier's thirst.

She found a pale and stricken foe,
  Sinking in nature's last eclipse,
And on the red earth kneeling low,
  She wet his parch'd and fever'd lips ;
When, thick as winter's driving sleet,
  The booming shot and flaming shell
Swept with wild rage that gory street,
  And she — the good and gentle — fell !

They laid her in her narrow bed —
  The foemen of her land and race ;
And sighs were breathed and tears were shed
  Above her lowly resting-place.
Ay ! glory's crimson worshippers
  Wept over her unkindly fall,
For deeds of mercy such as hers
  Subdue the heart and eyes of all.

To sound her worth were guilt and shame
  In us, who love but gold and ease ;
They heed alike our praise or blame,
  Who live and die in works like these,

Far greater than the wise or brave,
    Far happier than the fair or gay,
Was she who found a martyr's grave
    On that red field of Monterey.

—Rev. J. G. Lyons.

Zachary Taylor,

The Whigs were now beginning to want a hand in the government. They had been out of power so long, that they thought it worth while to try to find a man as their candidate who would be likely to catch the vote of the people.

They settled upon "Old Zach," or as he had come to be called during the late war, "Old Rough and Ready." This wasn't as exciting a time as that campaign when Log Cabins and Hard Cider had been the campaign watch-words; but it was somewhat like it. Now everything was "Rough and Ready," — there were "Rough and Ready" hats and "Rough and Ready" boots — and at the end, the Whigs, to their great delight, succeeded in electing their "Rough and Ready" president. President Taylor died before his term of office was ended, and his Vice-President, Millard Filmore, served the remainder of the term. After Filmore came Franklin Pierce, and after Pierce, James Buchanan.

ZACARY TAYLOR

The administrations of these presidents are so swallowed up in the great question of "slavery," that I shall not try to keep them separate in this little history. You have heard already of the slavery question, but you did not know, I think, how in all this time the excitement regarding it had been increasing. The political parties which in Washington's time were divided on the form of government, and later, on the war with England, and later still, on "State Rights," were now divided on the one great question of slavery. For some time, whenever a new territory wanted to join the Union, there had been a hot fight in Congress over it. The question would be, not whether there were people enough in the territory, or whether they would be likely to be of service to the Union, but, "Will this new State be a slave-state?" If it seemed likely that it would be a slave-state, then the North would fight against its admission. They wanted no more slave-states. On the other hand, if it was not to be a slave-state, the South would fight just as hotly against it.

Away back when South Carolina had made an attempt to leave the Union, and "Old Hickory" had brought it so quickly to terms, he had said then, — wise, far seeing old man that he was:

"This disturbance about the tariff is only a make believe; the real object in trying to withdraw from the Union is to secure the right to hold slaves. Slavery, or the Negro Question, will be the next trouble this country will have to face."

And surely enough his prophecy was coming true. Henry Clay and Daniel Webster worked harder than ever in these days; for the South again had threatened to leave the Union — this time making no pretence to keep back their real object, the slave question.

FRANKLIN PIERCE

MILLARD FILLMORE

JAMES BUCHANAN

The Abolitionists.

Another long word, children; but as very likely your own grandfather was an abolitionist himself in those days, you will want to know what the word means.

We are now close upon the terrible war which was brought about by this disagreement between the North and the South, The Abolitionists — that is, the people who believed in doing away with slavery — had come to be quite large in number. The North had all these years believed that slavery was not right; and while they had done away with it in their own States, they had not pushed very hard in the matter against the South. But now the Abolitionists had come. They not only *believed* that slavery was wrong, but they were determined it should be abolished.

The Southerners hated and feared these Abolitionists. " What if they should come here among our slaves and teach them about liberty and freedom ! " said they.

The first Abolitionist of the times was Benjamin Lunday, one of the good old Pennsylvania Quakers. He began talking up this matter with everybody he met, till at last his name and his sayings began to be talked about in the newspapers ; other newspapers took it up, and others, and others, — some praising the good Quaker, others condemning him. But whether they praised or condemned, they set people all over the country to thinking, and many a one who had never given it a thought before, began now to wonder in their own minds if the Quaker wasn't right, after all.

Benjamin Lunday came to Boston at length; and there he found William Lloyd Garrison, who was as full of the desire to see the slaves free as he was himself.

And such talk and such excitement as these two men did stir up in good old Boston! There had been nothing like it since the old Revolutionary times. Garrison went to work and published a newspaper called the "Liberator," in which he set forth freely his opinions on the slavery question. The whole country was set boiling by this paper. His very life was in danger. In one State, five thousand dollars were offered for his head.

The people of Boston itself threatened to tar and feather him if he did not hold his peace. "I am right, and I will speak!" was his answer. At last he was seized by a mob, and dragged about the streets by a rope. I don't know what would have become of him had not the mayor of the city come to his rescue. He was put in jail that he might be safe from the mob.

Out in Illinois, another newspaper editor was doing the same sort of work. He, too, was mobbed, his presses destroyed, and he himself killed in the fray.

All this time the little party of men and women who called themselves Abolitionists were growing stronger and stronger. And now when the news of this murder reached the ears of the Boston Abolitionists, a meeting was called in the old "Cradle of Liberty."

And it was at this meeting that Wendell Phillips, the silver-tongued orator, first came into notice. He was young, and rich, and educated, belonging to the very best families in Massachusetts, having everything in his favor whereby to make for himself a high place in the world. But all this he threw aside, and came and joined the little band of despised Abolitionists, joining with William Lloyd Garrison as a leader in the cause of freedom for the negroes.

At the same time, our dear old Quaker poet, as he is called now, joined the ranks. He was young then, and was just beginning to come into notice among the people of the land. He, too, had a life of ease and glory before him if only he had not taken up the slavery question; but when he began to plead for the poor negro of the South through his beautiful verses, just as Wendell Phillips was pleading for them from the platform, then the people turned against him as they had turned against Wendell Phillips; and for thirty years this poet whom now we all love so much, and regard with such tender reverence, was looked upon with contempt, and was insulted and scoffed at by the people. Dear, tender-hearted Whittier! Are not you glad, children, that he has lived to see the day when his countrymen do love him as he deserved? What do you

John G. Whittier

suppose the people in those Abolition days would have said if some one had told them that in less than thirty years John G. Whittier's verses would be in all our books, and better still, in all our hearts; and that the children all over the country would be celebrating this self-same Whittier's birthdays in their school-rooms, reading and speaking and singing of the "gentle Quaker poet?"

THE FUGITIVE SLAVE LAW.

Sometimes these slaves used to run away. If they could get into the Northern States, that is, into the free states, they themselves were free. Of course this did not please the slave owners; and so Henry Clay, who as we have heard before, was always presenting some sort of a bill in Congress that served to keep the North and South from an actual quarrel, brought before the Senate a law which was called "The Fugitive Slave Law." Fugitive means run-away — and by means of this new law, a slave holder was given the right to pursue a runaway slave into any State, and bring him back. This law seemed all right at first, and no doubt Henry Clay meant that it should be all right. At any rate, he brought it before the Senate at a time when the South would, but for this law, have broken out in open rebellion.

This proved to be a very cruel law however, for the slave holders, some of them wicked and hard-hearted, would pursue their runaway slaves just as they would have pursued runaway cattle, and would drive them home with the lash. Some of the slaves so dreaded to go back, that when they found their masters were coming for them, they would kill themselves rather than be taken. Sometimes mothers would kill their little children rather than they should grow up slaves.

Let me tell you here the story of Margaret Garner, as Abbey Sage Richardson tells it in her history of our country.

"Margaret was a slave. Not a very black slave, but with a dusky yellow skin like those we call mulattoes. She had two children, a boy and girl. The little girl was white, as fair, perhaps, as you or I. From some cause or other, Margaret Garner did not like to stay in slavery, and ran away with her two children and two other slaves. They all hid in the house of a free negro, but were soon tracked to their hiding-place by Margaret's master and a force of men he had brought with him. The door was barred, but the officers battered it down and got in. When they entered, there stood Margaret Garner with a bloody knife in her hand between the bodies of her two children. She had cut their throats with her own hand, and said that she would rather have them dead than taken back to slavery. The little girl was already quite dead, but the boy was only wounded and afterwards got well. Margaret loved her dead baby, called her " Birdie," and wept when she told how pretty she was. But so far as I can learn she never was sorry that she killed her. They carried the mother and her wounded boy back to her master, and she was never heard of any more."

It was in these exciting times that Charles Sumner, a man as great as Daniel Webster, made his noted speeches in the Senate on the question of slavery.

So enraged was one of the Southern congressmen at something he had said, that he attacked Sumner while sitting at his desk, beat him over the head with his cane until the grand old senator fell senseless upon the floor.

And what do you think was done about this cowardly act? Oh, nothing at all. The North was furious; indignation meetings were held, and hundreds and hundreds of Northerners joined the Abolitionists. But the South honored this man for what he had done, considered it a pretty smart thing, and sent him another and a stronger cane with the hope that he would use it again if opportunity came.

John Brown

I wonder if you have any idea, when you sing that old song about "John Brown's body," what it all means. I'm sure I didn't know when I was a child, and I can remember just how I used to enjoy singing it at the top of my voice ! Let me see — it goes something like this, doesn't it?

> John Brown's body lies a' mouldering in the grave,
> John Brown's body lies a' mouldering in the grave,
> John Brown's body lies a' mouldering in the grave,
> But his soul goes marching on.
> Glory, glory hallelujah, etc.

JOHN BROWN.

There was a great struggle going on in Kansas between the people in it who believed in slavery and the people in it who did not believe in slavery.

Soldiers had even been sent to Kansas from the South to

try to subdue the Free-State people. Four or five hundred
of these soldiers came to Ossawatomie, where John Brown
lived, for the purpose of attacking the town.   John Brown
had only thirty men to meet this force with, and so could
not expect to be victorious ; but so skilfully did he manage
his thirty, that he led them to a safe retreat with the loss
of only five or six, while the enemy lost thirty-one and had
more than twice that number wounded, beside having had a
close, hard fight.   After that, John Brown was always
called "Ossawatomie Brown ;" and when the town was
besieged a second time, the citizens sent for Ossawatomie
Brown to defend them.   He came with his little band,
never more than thirty or forty, and made it so hot for
the enemy that they went away without giving battle.

John Brown stood bravely by the Kansas Free-State citizens until the time came when they were strong enough to
defend themselves.   He now prepared to go away.   Just
as he was ready to go, a slave came to him begging him to
assist him to escape with his wife and children.   You may
be sure that no appeal from slaves was, by brave John Brown,
unheeded.   Not only did he assist this slave, but he also
marched boldly over into the plantation where the slave
lived, killed the master, took twelve other slaves, and
helped them all to Canada, where they were out of reach of
United States law.   Of course this act brought down the
wrath of the South upon him, and he was no longer safe in

that part of the country. And so it was well that he, too, escaped with the slaves into Canada. A few months later there came into Virginia a white-haired old man with some younger men who were said to be his sons. These men hired a farm near Harper's Ferry, and set to work upon it. They received a great many boxes and packages by rail, which they said were their farming tools.

HARPER'S FERRY.

At Harper's Ferry was an arsenal, stored with guns and powder, and all the munitions of war. One night, as the three watchmen were guarding the gates, up marched a company of twenty-two men. In a twinkling the three watchmen were seized, and bound hand and foot; then the twenty-two march in and took possession of the arsenal.

Now you have guessed who this white-haired farmer with his sons is! John Brown, of course; but what is he going to do? Simply this: he is going to prepare for war against slavery. It seems at first absurd that a little band of twenty-two should set themselves up against a nation; but they were stronger than they seemed. Already his allies outside had cut down the telegraph wires, and had torn up the railroads, so that news of their deed could not spread over the country.

Out into the town John Brown and his men marched, taking prisoner every citizen they met.

"What does this mean?" the astonished prisoners would say.

"It means that we are going to free the slaves!" answered John Brown.

"In whose name do you do this?"

"Not in the name of Congress, but in the name of Almighty God."

John Brown had made arrangements with, and was expecting a band of a hundred slaves to join him as soon as they should know that the arsenal was taken. For some unknown reason, these slaves did not appear. He waited for them until too late. By noon, a company of militia marched to the arsenal, and now all hope of escape was cut off. By evening, fifteen hundred soldiers had arrived, and a bloody contest followed. John Brown's men knew, of course, that their doom was sealed, but they fought like tigers to the very last.

At night the party in the arsenal numbered only seven, and three of those were sorely wounded. All night long John Brown sat upon the floor between his two sons, one dead, the other slowly dying. At daybreak the door was broken in, and the soldiers were in the presence of this old hero, John Brown.

As soon as their eyes fell upon this daring man, one officer struck him over the head with his sabre, and another cruelly speared him in the side.

And so ended "John Brown's Raid" as it was called. He was tried by the Virginia court, and sentenced to be hanged. He was very brave and noble during the time he lay in prison, and when the day on which he was to be hanged came, he was calm and full of courage. He felt that he had done only what was right. "I have broken the laws of the State," said he; but "I have kept the laws of God; and the laws of God are greater than any laws of State."

As he walked forth from his jail on this last morning of his life, there stood at the gateway a slave woman with her baby in her arms.   As he passed her he stooped and kissed the baby, and then went on, sadly but quietly.   The little black baby did not know what a friend this old man was to him, nor did he know that he was giving his life for him, but the mother knew ; and I hope she lived to be free and to know that this old hero did not give his life in vain.

On the scaffold he was blindfolded and led out upon the drop.   For ten minutes he was kept standing there, expecting every second to hear the death signal.   There seemed little need of this last stroke of cruelty ; and even the mob about the scaffold began at last to cry, " shame ! " " shame ! " Then the drop fell, and John Brown was dead.

Don't you think now we ought to finish up this second volume of our history with a song.   I do ; and I think the song ought to be about this brave old man who took his stand against the buying and selling of God's children, as if they had been sheep and oxen, away back in the early days of the anti-slavery excitement, before there were many people to aid him or to even give him a word of sympathy in his efforts.

BROWN OF OSSAWATOMIE.

JohnBrown of Ossawatomie spake on his dying day :
" I will not have to shrive my soul a priest in Slavery's pay.

But let some poor slave-mother whom I have striven to free,
With her children, from the gallows' stair put up a prayer for
    me ! "

John Brown of Ossawatomie, they led him out to die ;
And lo ! a poor slave-mother with her little child pressed nigh.
Then the bold, blue eye grew tender, and the old harsh face grew
    mild,
As he stooped between the jeering ranks and kissed the negro's
    child !
The shadows of his stormy life that moment fell apart ;
And they who blamed the bloody hand forgave the loving heart.
That kiss from all its guilty means redeemed the good intent,
And round the grisly fighter's hair the martyr's aureole bent !

Perish with him the folly that seeks through evil good !
Long live the generous purpose unstained with human blood !
Not the raid of midnight terror, but the thought which underlies ;
Not the borderer's pride of daring, but the Christian's sacrifice.

Nevermore may yon Blue Ridges the Northern rifle hear,
Nor see the light of blazing homes flash on the negro's spear.
But let the free-winged angel, Truth, their guarded passes scale,
To teach that right is more than might, and justice more than mail !

So vainly shall Virginia set her battle in array ;
In vain her trampling squadrons knead the winter snow with clay.
She may strike the pouncing eagle, but she dares not harm the
    dove ;
And every gate she bars to Hate shall open wide to Love !
                    —J. G. WHITTITR.

A New Order of the Ages
The true story and meaning of the
Great Seal of the United States

In recent years, many historians have insisted that the American Founding Fathers were deists. A deist is someone who believes that God created the universe and then walked away from it, never to care for it or give it a second thought. I vividly remember being taught this very thing in public school, and at the time, had no reason to question it.

When I started reading our history for myself (from original sources) I was surprised to learn that such was not the case. The Founding Fathers were profoundly religious. In their own words they state unapologetically that freedom comes from God and that it was He who directed them to build this nation. They understood the Bible as the history of man's struggle for freedom, first from the tyrannical king of Egypt, then from the wages of Sin and Death through the liberation of Jesus Christ and lastly from the chains of Great Britain.

George Washington prayed frequently for divine guidance. One of his prayers has come down to us: "Let my heart, gracious God, be so affected with Your glory and majesty that I may fulfill these weighty duties which you require of me. Again, I have called you for pardon and forgiveness of sins and for the sacrifice of Jesus Christ offered on the cross for me. You gave your Son to die for me and have given me assurance of salvation." Once when Thomas Jefferson was asked his opinion of religion, he stated. "The genuine and simple religion of Jesus will one day be restored: such as it was preached and practiced by Himself." Jefferson also taught, "The First Amendment has erected a wall of separation between church and state. That wall is a one dimensional wall. It keeps government from running the church, but it makes sure that Christian principles will always stay in government." These are hardly the words of deists.

In drafting our Constitution, James Madison declared, "We have staked the whole future of American civilization not upon the power of government. We have staked the future of all our political constitutions upon the capacity of each and all of us to govern ourselves according to the Ten Commandments of God." These are a few quotes of many.

In order to safeguard these ideals and place them forever before the people, it was decided that a seal (or coat of arms) should be given to the new nation. Thus begins the real meaning behind the symbols found on the Great Seal of the United States.

On July 4, 1776, our Founding Fathers gathered at Independence Hall to sign the Declaration of Independence. Shortly after the committee passed the following resolution: "Dr. Franklin, Mr. J. Adams and Mr. Jefferson, be a committee, to bring in a device for a seal for the United States of America." These three gentlemen sought the advice of a coat of arms scholar, Pierre Eugène Du Simitière. Over the next six years, the Great Seal was designed. Since that day, many uneducated, but well-meaning scholars, have attached various and sundry sinister meanings to our national coat of arms. The real meaning behind these symbols is one of God-fearing faith and hope for man's future.

Our national coat of arms is made up of two symbols. First, a bald eagle with wings outstretched. The eagle symbolizes strength, victory and safety. The concept is similar to the idea John the Revelator portrayed in his Apocalypse (see KJV Revelation 12:10-14).

The eagle bears a shield of 13 stripes and stars on its chest. He clutches an olive branch in one talon and 13 arrows in the other. The eagle always faces the olive branch but keeps the arrows close by. This symbol is meant as a promise and a warning to the world. It means that America prefers peace. We will look to peace first, however, if necessary, we will defend our rights, our prosperity and our peace with war.

Overhead, 13 heavenly stars unitedly let their light so shine among men, that the good works of freedom can be seen by all. The eagle clutches a ribbon in his break with a Latin inscription translated as, "From the many people, come one." This echoes Jesus's teaching, "If ye are not one, ye are not mine."

The second symbol is the all-seeing eye of God shining above a pyramid of 13 steps. God's watchful eye is gazing down upon the 13 colonies from His place in the heavens. Above the eye is the pronouncement, "God favors our undertaking." The eye is set in a triangle symbolizing the three members of the Trinity. This triangle is also meant to form a capstone at the head of a corner. Jesus once declared that the stone which the builder's rejected, the same has become the head of the corner. Our founders believed that it was God's will that America be free.

The pyramid's foundation is inscribed with Roman numerals signifying the year 1776. The western side of the pyramid is dark suggesting that while our future is still unknown to man, it is known to God. It also declares that the original 13 colonies would expand westward in *manifest destiny* until freedom filled the whole earth.

Perhaps nothing in urban mythology has so inspired panic as the remaining Latin phrase, "Novus Ordo Seclorum." There are those who claim it is the secret saying of a group of power hungry socialists who hope to take over the world. Perhaps so. Human history is filled with Hitlers, Lenins, Darwins and other social architects and fools. Our Founding Fathers had a different vision of these words. They read them as, "A new order of the Ages." They saw America as the start of a new order for the world. A new way of life built here in the pristine forests of the American continent. In a world accustomed to the old order of kings and servants, monarchs and subjects, masters and slaves, this new order of individual freedom was dangerous and unstoppable. It still is.

As the years have passed, America has continued to inspire hope to the huddled masses of humanity yearning to be free. Our influence has expanded through peace and through war. We have saved the human race in two world wars, defeated global communism and aided developing nations in the principles of freedom. We have out lasted monarchs, tyrants and despots. God has truly favored our endeavors and blessed mankind with a new order for living. He has given us every reason to push forward blending the many peoples and cultures into one people, a free people... we the people.

May the love of liberty shine bright within you, and may the Author of it bless this nation, now and always. - Reed R. Simonsen

If you enjoyed these stories of our heritage, you will love the stories of our Revolution. *American History Stories... you never read in school Volume I: The Shot Heard 'Round the World* contains numerous stories of the brave men, women and children who gave their all that we might be free. Ask for ISBN: 0-9640546-0-4.

Also visit our web site for more patriotic stories and gems: http://homepage.mac.com/randallco.

If you would like to receive additional copies of our books for personal, promotional, educational or other reasons, please inquire at your local bookstore, visit our website or write to:

> The Randall Company
> P.O. Box 291
> Centerville, Utah 84014

Those wishing to obtain prints of Tom Freeman's patriotic works may call 1-888-215-9403 or write to:

> SM&S Naval Prints, Inc.
> P.O. Box 41
> Forest Hill, MD 21050-0041